THE JAGUAR XJ40 PROJECT

Papers presented at a seminar sponsored by
The Automobile Division of
The Institution of Mechanical Engineers

28 August 1986

The Institution of Mechanical Engineers
Birdcage Walk
London

Published for
The Institution of Mechanical Engineers
by Mechanical Engineering Publications Limited
LONDON

THE JAGUAR XJ4O PROJECT

Printed and Distributed

by SAE®

in North America

400 Commonwealth Drive, Warrendale, PA 15096

ISBN 0 85298 619 X

The papers contained in this volume were first published in the *Proceedings of the Institution of Mechanical Engineers, Part D,* 1986

Printed by Moreton Hall Press Ltd, Bury St Edmunds.

CONTENTS

The design and development of a new luxury sector automobile

J N Randle, CEng, FIMechE, FInstD
Jaguar Cars Limited, Coventry

This paper describes the programme of design and development undertaken during the production of the a luxury automobile, the Jaguar XJ40.

1 INTRODUCTION

Since its inception Jaguar has traditionally aimed its product at the specialist and luxury sectors.

In 1980 when work began in earnest on this project, the company was in a parlous state. The combination of a second fuel crisis, a bad reputation for reliability and quality and a cost structure incompatible with the volumes of vehicles being produced, added up to a company which was rapidly going out of business.

The BL Board's decision to support the XJ40 project, under the direction of Sir Michael Edwardes, was at that time a considerable act of faith. The urgency of the situation pertaining at that time was towards the production of lightweight, highly efficient, highly economical vehicles. Indeed there were many predictions that cars above two litre capacity would have no future.

However, the company's own research, particularly in the American market, led to the belief that this was not in fact the case and that the primary objectives needed to be towards improvement in reliability, quality and value for money, while maintaining the company's position in the market place. Indeed, with the general downsizing of American cars there was a strong possibility that what was hitherto a relatively small car would be seen by the American public as being more in line with luxury car perceptions.

It was against this background that the programme laid before the BL Board in May 1980 had the following principal objectives:

1. To reduce manufacturing complexity and thereby improve productivity and quality.
2. To improve reliability through improved standards and procedures.
3. To improve economy through low weight, improved aerodynamics and improved engine and engine management and transmission management systems.
4. To achieve a better performance and to maintain the car's position in the luxury sector by at least equalling its predecessor in style and refinement.

A number of important and far-reaching decisions had to be made, most of which demanded a compromise between one requirement or another. These involved:

1. Exterior style, which would require a careful trade-off between traditional Jaguar elegance and low drag aerodynamics and aerodynamic stability.
2. Interior style where traditional virtues of wood, chrome and leather had to be weighed against the incorporation of new technologies.
3. The desire to widen the owner profile without disaffecting the traditional Jaguar owner.

Economy had to be judged against the refinement targets, since weight reduction inevitably places substantial difficulties in the way of noise attenuation.

Reliability would not have to be compromised in order to reduce weight; yet against this it was vitally necessary that the new car complied with North American 'gas guzzler' fuel economy targets.

Cost targets again presented restraints against the achievement of reliability and quality targets.

Features had to meet the highest levels of competition, while maintaining weight and cost targets.

Timing was a substantial problem. The state of the company was such that the production of the new car in the shortest possible time was imperative, and yet the limited resource that was available was already directed towards resolving the quality and reliability problems being experienced with the current product.

Finally, there was the method by which the vehicle should be designed and developed. Should it be entirely computer aided designed? Should it be entirely rig tested or should it be road and track tested in the conventional manner? Should new methods of road load data collection and fatigue prediction be introduced?

The following detailed descriptions indicate the methods and solutions that were applied to solve these questions.

2 EXTERIOR STYLE

Style and elegance has always been of central importance to the company's products. The legacy of Sir William Lyons has been a series of beautiful cars whose style has impressed itself on the minds of the motoring public for over two generations. It is worth tracing some of that style back to the late 1950s, in order to see how the XJ40 style has been generated.

2.1 Mark IX

This aristocratic car (Fig. 1) was launched in 1958 with a blanked radiator coefficient of 0.39. (It is useful to quote blanked radiator figures in all cases since this

Fig. 1 Mark IX

Fig. 3 Mark X

gives a truer indication of the basic aerodynamic form drag of the vehicle.) Here, the now-distinctive Jaguar saloon styling first began to emerge; note especially the rounded paw-like qualities of the front wings and the beginnings of the characteristic radiator and protruberant headlamps simulating a face.

2.2 Mark II

The Mark II (Fig. 2), the businessman's express, was launched in 1959 with a blanked radiator drag coefficient of 0.38. An outstandingly successful and beautiful car, it clearly established the company's position as a class leader in terms of value for money, performance, state-of-the-art handling, high-quality interior appointments and distinctive exterior styling.

Particular note had been made of the front and front wings, a theme which Sir William established and was to work with subtle variations for the rest of his career.

2.3 Mark X

The Mark X (Fig. 3), launched in 1964, had a blanked radiator drag coefficient of 0.395. The front end had developed somewhat from the earlier cars and in some ways was slightly more drag provoking, but in spite of the somewhat large size of this vehicle, it was still clearly a Jaguar and Sir William's genius for holding a theme while permitting change is very evident in this car.

2.4 XJ series

The XJ6 launched in 1968 had a blanked radiator coefficient of 0.4. In styling terms Sir William achieved with the XJ series (Fig. 4) a successful synthesis of saloon and sports car themes, and here the subtle feline quality of the lines was matched by refined performance and a sure-footed ride and handling quality.

2.5 The styling decision

The choice for the XJ40 was therefore either a conservative evolutionary style, as had largely been the case with Sir William's saloons, or a more radical approach. In surveys and styling clinics conducted both in the UK, Europe and the USA it became very clear that a marked change in design philosophy would not be welcomed by the traditional customer body. It was therefore decided that the market place demanded a more evolutionary style, the targets being to show a clear evolution from the Series III but to have a lower Cd (drag coefficient) than the Series III and a better Cd than both the Series III and its competitors, while maintaining traditional stability levels.

With these requirements in mind, the drag-raising features of Series III were assessed using the MIRA (Motor Industry Research Association) rating method and a series of wind tunnel studies, which confirmed that the most distinctive feature of Jaguar styling, the front end, was responsible for the largest single contribution to the drag figure.

Many other features, for instance the canopy peak and plan form and rear boat tailing, were all good drag features. It was therefore decided that it was the front end of the car which required most attention.

Modifications chosen were to ease the forward slope of the radiator, to remove the eyebrows on the headlamps and to give a top-to-bottom radius on the front end corners. These would leave the general overall front end appearance largely unaltered but would address the major drag-raising aspects, without affecting the very good aerodynamic stability achieved by the current car.

Wind tunnel work was carried out on a full-scale fibreglass model in the conventional way. As is well known, unblanked radiator drag can be reduced by fitting an airdam or front spoiler which works by speeding up the airflow in the engine compartment, thereby reducing pressure on the rearward-facing areas and reducing front end lift.

Fig. 2 Mark II

Fig. 4 XJ series

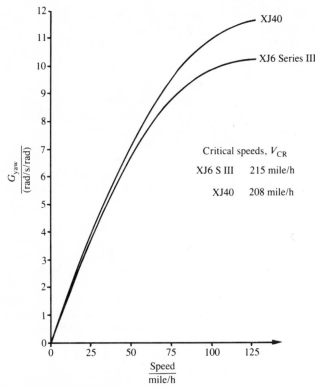

Fig. 5 Yaw gain versus speed (G_{yaw} = yaw angular speed/ unit steer angle)

Rear end lift is often reduced by the addition of a spoiler. Needless to say, a large fixed additive rear spoiler was not considered an acceptable styling feature on a Jaguar saloon. A compromise, and visually attractive solution, was the incorporation of a small boot lid lip. A detailed study was conducted to optimize front spoiler depth and rake and boot lip size and angle, which in combination minimized unblanked radiator drag and kept the front and rear lift distribution in the desired range. The objective had been to improve the drag, that is Cds below the Series III, and to be better than the current competition.

The results were:

XJ40	0.762
Series III	0.849
Competitor A	0.8748
Competitor B	0.8103

The cross-wind stability remained the equal of Series III while being better than the competition (Fig. 5).

3 OCCUPANT ENVIRONMENT

The occupant's response to the vehicle is governed by many complex and inter-related experiences—tactile, acoustic, ergonomic and visual.

Substantial programmes of work were undertaken in all of these areas to try to produce an experience that in total would be better than both the company's current vehicles and the competitors' vehicles.

3.1 Interior style

One's first impressions on entering a new car are visual. Jaguar's traditional virtues of wood, leather and chrome seem at first to be at odds with the adoption of new

technologies and the desire to manufacture the vehicle in a more cost effective and productive way.

The generation of a style which would achieve all of these ends was perhaps the most difficult process in the whole of the project's development. It involved many reiterations and clinic reappraisals before a style was achieved which satisfied all owners, both current and prospective, and trod the finely balanced line between the traditional and the technically advanced.

The outcome is an interior trim system which uses both the latest production technologies and traditional materials in a sympathetic way, allowing craftsmanship to be used where it is seen and employing modern technologies in areas that are not visible to the occupants.

3.2 Air conditioning (1)

The condition of the air surrounding the driver has most important effects upon his or her comfort and alertness.

Before embarking on a programme to design a new air conditioning unit, it was necessary to determine the exact requirements by surveying competitors' performances and customers' needs, and by examining the physiological requirements of the human body. Air flow, temperature ranges and humidity levels had to be determined.

The objectives were quite clear:

1. To improve performance over current cars and potential competitors.
2. To increase reliability over potential competitors.
3. To reduce weight against current units.
4. To maintain or reduce existing package size.

In order to achieve these objectives, it was necessary to describe the unit in engineering terms. The specification which was produced was a far-reaching document that covered all areas of the unit's performance, quality, reliability, weight and noise. Every attempt was made in the preparation of the document to prevent errors and to make interpretation absolutely clear. The process demanded full failure modes and effects analysis and process controls to levels far in excess of anything we had attempted before.

The design that resulted from these specifications is unusual in that it uses two rotary air valves to achieve the air mixing. These are controlled entirely electronically through a closed-loop system which measures the position of the flap and feeds that information back to a controlling microprocessor.

The heater and evaporator matrices are conventional, but the unit is unconventional in that it controls humidity by way of independent control of the 'air off' temperature of the matrix; in this way it controls the water vapour content of the air entering the vehicle.

The unit is designed to give satisfactory levels of performance from +52 to −30°C; it requires an evaporative performance of 8.14 kW and a heating performance of 9.88 kW.

To produce the minimum disturbance from air speed changes the fans are controlled through a chopper system, giving infinitely variable speeds. In the automatic mode, sensing is through an aspirated thermistor with additional tuning from a solar sensor mounted near the front windshield.

Additional tuning is effected through a third thermistor mounted in the fan inlet to measure the incoming air temperature.

Since experience has shown that it is not possible to satisfy fully all conditions automatically, a manual mode is available which allows 'air off' temperature to be selected via the temperature control.

3.3 Driver information and control system (2)

The XJ40's position in the market place demanded a conservative and tasteful, yet technologically advanced, information system capable of displaying the ever-increasing number of warning functions demanded both by the market place and by legislative requirements. It must at the same time retain flexibility for change and be simple to control and understand. The design answer to this challenge was arrived at after careful examination of market demands, competitive trends and after evaluating the latest technology available from suppliers.

The solution chosen was to centre the information display in a single area using a 32 × 32 vacuum fluorescent dot matrix, with alphanumeric supplementary support (Fig. 6). The speedometer and tachometer were maintained as traditional needle instruments, while the continuous monitoring displays of oil pressure, battery state, water temperature and fuel level were vacuum fluorescent bar displays, which change colour when entering cautionary zones. As an additional alert system, the frames to the symbols alongside the bar graphs flash whenever the readout is in a critical zone. The dot matrix is capable of displaying any of the conventional ISO symbols plus a number of symbols which

were designed in order to alert the driver to various conditions requiring attention.

The design was submitted to an extensive evaluation programme which was conducted by the Institute of Consumer Ergonomics and involved a total of 600 drivers. As a result, various refinements were made and a system was created which has widespread acceptability. The trip computer controls were also subjected to the same appraisal system.

The final design which resulted from this work is a nine-key trip computer control panel which allows the driver to call up as much no-nonsense information as would sensibly be required. He or she can be informed of:

(a) the distance travelled,
(b) the distance to go,
(c) the range available in the fuel tank if the journey continued at the average speed that had been used up to the point of requiring the range,
(d) the fuel used during the journey,
(e) the instantaneous fuel consumption at any time,
(f) the average fuel consumption over the journey,
(g) the journey time taken,
(h) the estimated arrival time,
(i) the average speed for the journey.

All of the information provided appears in the alphanumeric display below the dot matrix symbol area, and not only indicates the values but also the information requested to avoid any possibility of misinterpretation.

3.4 Autoshift control

A gearbox with a high overdrive ratio, while giving good consumption figures, may not necessarily provide the most sporting characteristics. Since it was wished to exploit the performance potential of the car, the ability to operate the vehicle in a pseudo-manual mode was considered to be an advantage.

A gear change control design was therefore created which would achieve this but would be as free as possible from potential misuse. Many systems that encourage the easy use of the lower gear retention suffer from the possibility of inadvertent engagement of reverse, park or neutral when changing back to the normal D-mode. The provision of a reasonable separation between the functions helps to overcome this problem but unfortunately leads to a very long shift action. The simple expediency of bending the gate into the 'J' shape (Fig. 7) enabled both the problem of the lengthy action and the possibility of inadvertent mis-selection to be solved.

Fig. 6   Information display

Fig. 7   The 'J' gate

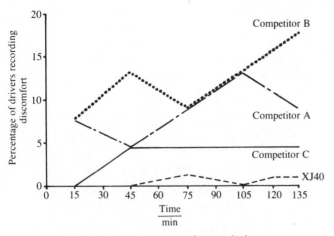

Fig. 8 Driver's seat comfort analysis

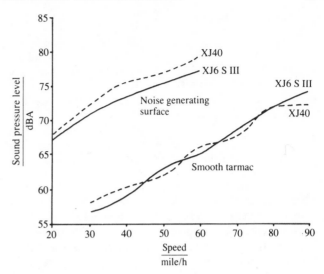

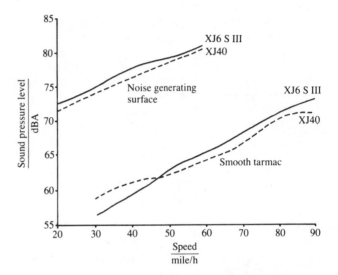

Fig. 9 A-weighted interior noise versus engine speed (a) front passenger and (b) rear passenger head positions

To ensure that the driver does not leave the gear lever in position other than the park mode, an audible warning sounds when the ignition key is withdrawn when the gear selector is in any position other than park. This system was again subjected to similar customer evaluation programmes to those used on the instrument display, the trip computer and the air conditioning control system.

3.5 Seating (3)

To design a seat which is acceptable to a wide range of drivers and passengers while maintaining traditional style and craftsmanship presented a difficult target. The seats fitted to the current range of vehicles had been developed to a good level of universal acceptability, following many years of development and attention to criticism from the market place. There was clearly, however, a need to go further in order to match the competition.

A worldwide literature survey was carried out with the assistance of Loughborough University, from which an idealized seat design was created. This design was assessed through many clinics and driver test programmes and through a large number of iterations until a final design was achieved. The resulting design gave good results compared to the company's current seats and to current competition (see Fig. 8).

4 NOISE AND VIBRATION

To be acceptable to occupants, interior noise levels need to be sufficiently low to enable easy conversation at any vehicle speed, they should allow appreciation of the audio system and should vary uniformly with speed without peaks or hollows and should be pleasant. Vibration levels should be at a barely discernible level and again should be uniform with speed and free of harshness when traversing rough road surfaces or when the vehicle or engine is in the extremes of the operating range.

The detailed description of all of those parameters is exceedingly complex and has required attention to many areas of the body and suspension structure, as is outlined later in this paper.

In simple terms the XJ40 had to behave at least as well as the current vehicle, which is regarded by many as the best in the sector in this respect. How well that has been achieved can be judged by the response characteristics outlined in Fig. 9a and b.

The test procedures used are unique to Jaguar but are recognized accurate methods of judging refinement.

5 REFINEMENT, RIDE AND HANDLING

The methods by which acceptable ride and handling are combined with high levels of refinement are exceedingly complex and involves attention to all areas of the body structure and suspensions, tyre design, damper and mounting design etc. Despite the many developments in terms of computer analysis it is still, in our experience, a matter which requires careful and painstaking attention to detail. Almost every system in the vehicle will have an effect upon another system which still appears to require very many iterations before acceptable solutions can be found (4–6).

However, on the XJ40 many design solutions were applied to reduce this development process by the application of sound principles as follows.

5.1 Body structures (4)

A body structure is expensive, has long design and production lead times and is usually critical to the dynamic performance of the vehicle in all respects from handling to noise and vibration. It is therefore essential to establish the dynamic performance of the structure as early as possible in the development programme.

As Jaguar had previously worked with Birmingham University on the application of structural dynamic performance standards over a considerable period, their help was sought.

The system developed by Birmingham University, which involves the derivation of body modal parameters from the dynamic response of the structure, is a significant departure from traditional methods. By its use it is possible to assess a vehicle structure in terms of performance figures over a narrow or broad frequency bandwidth, taking into account the integrated effects of both resonant and non-resonant modes.

The performance standards used as benchmarks in this system have been determined after assessments of a large number of vehicle structures. As a result high confidence exists as to the reliability of the numbers used. The system involves testing using simple single-point forced vibrations, while measuring responses at a number of points on the vehicle structure, which is divided into approximately 70 elemental areas.

The responses of these areas are vectorially combined to form average frequency responses and thus the modal parameters of the structure are determined. By using this method a number of modifications were made. Structural members were redesigned and changes were made to the gauge of panels to ensure that the mass and stiffness of the structure was distributed to obtain optimum dynamic behaviour and ensure the minimization of problems in achieving the refinement levels sought in this project.

5.2 Suspension system

The suspension systems used in the current car have been widely acclaimed. Despite having been designed in the 1960s they can still be shown to have significant advantages over competitive systems devised in the 1980s. To achieve better suspension systems than those used in current cars required improvements in terms of handling, both steady state and transient, and ride comfort with particular respect to rear seat ride. There had to be better attenuation of axle noise, improved serviceability and, if possible, the system should be lighter and less expensive than current systems.

5.3 Front suspension

The current Series III system includes anti-dive geometry and uses the sub-frame for attenuating both road noise and engine noise, and as such has proven itself to be one of the most refined systems in use today. There seemed little to be gained by departing from this system and as a result the suspension system devised to replace it employs largely carry-over technology. However, there have been substantial detail changes designed to improve the efficiency of the suspension.

The most striking difference between the two suspen-

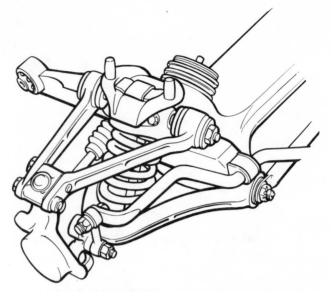

Fig. 10   Front suspension

sions is that the pitch control arms now face rearwards rather than forwards (see Fig. 10), anchoring into a stiffer part of the body structure, giving better steer control of the sub-frame. The beam itself is of much simpler construction than the Series III beam; it employs two major pressings thus reducing the part count to a minimum.

All the fulcrums and mounting points are machined after assembly, thus ensuring greater accuracy and eliminating the need for adjustment of camber or steering rack height. The suspension uprights are one-piece, again minimizing variations and ensuring that the steering rack ball joints are held to close height tolerances thus eliminating the need for rack height adjustment.

As with the Series III suspension, the dampers go directly to the body structure to ensure that the beam mounting system sees the suspension damping forces and therefore ensures good system control. The results of the design can be seen by reference to Fig. 11a and b indicating the performance relative to the current Series III systems.

5.4 Rear suspension (5)

In the design of the rear suspension system there has been a substantial departure from current practice (see Fig. 12a and b). Anti-dive and anti-squat were believed necessary in order to minimize system momentum by eliminating pitch changes during accelerating and braking. These in turn eliminate camber thrust changes and any bump steer effects that might exist within the geometry.

This has been achieved by inclining the inner wishbones to an angle of 8° which gives anti-squat compensation of 69 per cent and anti-dive compensation of 19 per cent. To eliminate the steer that results from inclining the wishbone on a twin-link system, the outer fulcrums were rotated through a further $4\frac{1}{2}°$ (see Fig. 12b), which introduces a compensating steer to the inner fulcrum inclination steer and ensures that the wheels point along the fore and aft axis at all times.

Improving the isolation beyond that achieved on current suspensions required the introduction of sub-

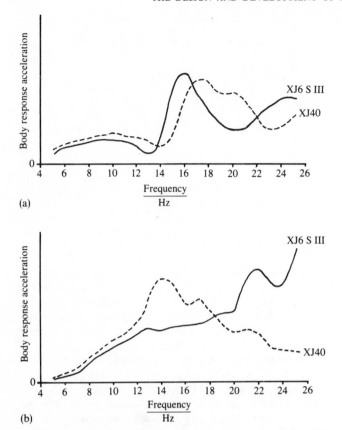

Fig. 11 Body response to suspension input (a) front and (b) rear

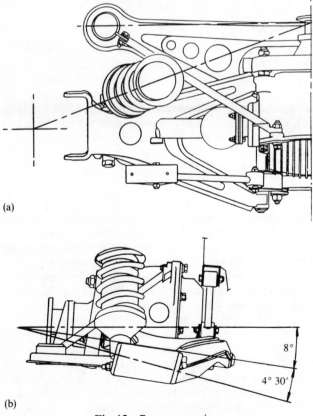

Fig. 12 Rear suspension

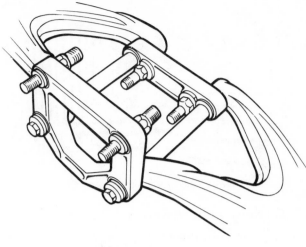

Fig. 13 Compliant system

stantial compliance in the fore and aft direction. This ensures that the fore and aft resonance of the wheel system is below wheel bounce frequency but yet allows the system to be compliant in all traction conditions other than at full throttle in first gear. Such low stiffness has been achieved without any loss of stiffness in the cornering force direction by the introduction of a pendulum ring at the front fulcrum and a compound beam at the rear fulcrum (Fig. 13).

The compliant system attaches to the axle which then allows the use of the axle mass as a road noise attenuator. Dampers and springs are mounted to the body structure in such a way as to provide a fulcrum to introduce a downthrust at the differential nose during weight transfer. This has the effect of reducing wind-up and allows a lower vertical mounting stiffness to be employed. As a result both road isolation and axle noise isolation are better while providing some system damping by way of suspension dampers in a similar manner to that used in the front suspension.

Outboard brakes were chosen although at first there was concern that the lowered unsprung weight could produce a handling problem. However, it was shown that the resultant lowered wheel bounce frequency improves the shake response by moving the wheel bounce mode frequencies away from the body beam-bending mode frequencies. This also has the effect of improving serviceability and reliability by reducing the heat input to the axle system. Camber changes were settled at three-quarters of the roll change, with minimum camber change at normal ride height, to minimize precessional effects and to optimize handling in the steady and transient states, where camber thrusts can be a problem.

The whole system is mounted in such a way that the load reaction line is as low as possible, using a frame mounted below the axle and connecting to the body longitudinal members at the front by way of a pair of inclined links at the rear of the axle, converging at the same height as the front mountings (Fig. 14). The overall result of this design has been a system which allows the use of ideal spring rates for both compliance, axle noise control and handling without introducing levels of compromise frequently found in competitive systems.

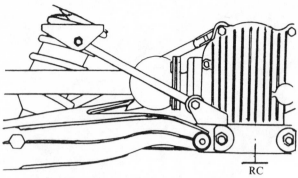

Fig. 14   Rear suspension mounting

5.5 The engine mounting system

Good design practice demands that engine mountings are placed at the nodes for the prime bending resonance of the engine/gearbox unit. This is not always possible and there is often a particular problem at the rear end of the gearbox. This was the case with the XJ40 which required the solution described later in this paper.

The point about which the mountings should act should be the point of minimum stiffness, which should coincide with the axis of minimum inertia. This will typically be high at the front of the engine, will pass through the centre of gravity and will be below the output flange at the rear of a six-cylinder in-line engine.

On the XJ40 the front engine mounts align with the front node, which is also on the front axle centre-line, the position of the two points being important in ensuring that there is no steer due to accelerative forces experienced at the engine mounts on a beam-mounted system.

Since the AJ6 engine is not vertical, a symmetrical solution was not possible. The solution nevertheless had to achieve the requirements of similar torsional stiffness from each mounting, with a stiffness centre in the horizontal plane below the axis of minimum inertia. Stiffness ratios were required which would give roll resonance below single-cylinder misfire frequency at tickover and a second pitch resonance sufficiently above wheel bounce to attenuate body movements at wheel bounce frequencies. It also had to have sufficient damping to attenuate the peak amplitudes seen at the second pitch resonance.

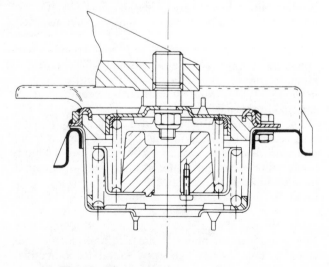

Fig. 15   The rear engine mounting system

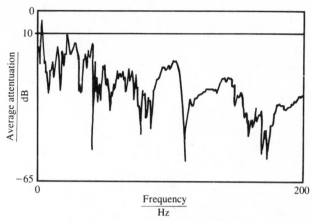

Fig. 16   Rear engine mounting transfer function

To achieve this a computer program was constructed which examined all of the possible solutions. Only one was ultimately practical, giving a starboard angle of 43°35′ with a stiffness ratio of 17.5 : 1 and a shore hardness of 55 and a port angle of 60°15′ with a stiffness ratio of 25 : 1 and a shore hardness of 60.

The rear engine mounting presented a more serious problem in that packaging constraints ensured that the mounting was almost at an anti-node and therefore had to have very high levels of attenuation. To achieve this a mass attenuating design was achieved which is resonant at 30 Hz and therefore gives attenuation at frequencies above 42 Hz (Fig. 15). Lateral control is achieved through a polyurethane ring designed to produce a rising rate with increasing lateral g. Rebound control is through the polyurethane pad over the gearbox. The attenuation achieved by this system is very high as is indicated in Fig. 16.

5.6 Dampers

The damper type employed allows the use of large differentials between bump and rebound, which is utilized to give good control while allowing a comfortable ride. To achieve the high levels of refinement and noise isolation required involved considerable attention to blow-off characteristics and friction content, employing a painstaking subjective, iterative process unchanged over several years.

5.7 Tyres

In developing a new tyre it was paramount that the comfort levels for which the current vehicle is renowned should not be lost. At the same time it was necessary to improve ultimate cornering power and response, coupled to which improved safety features were highly desirable. A development exercise was undertaken with two companies, which ultimately produced a 65 section tyre with bead locking and some run-flat capability.

Lower aspect ratio tyre sections generally improve handling and response but to the detriment of ride. In the development that was undertaken the rim bead height was reduced to maintain the side-wall section height, and hence comfort, while maintaining the bead–breaker height and breaker width, thus maintaining the improved handling that was sought.

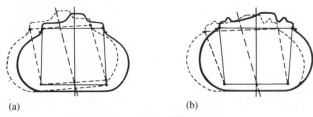

(a)   (b)

Fig. 17 Trapezoidal deflection

The reduced rim bead height resulted from the adoption of a locking toe system for bead retention, which was developed to maintain bead contact even in the event of total loss of pressure.

As a further development towards the combination of ride and handling, a relationship between the bead width and the breaker width was developed which is in essence trapezoidal. Under the effects of cornering the inner shoulder is pushed on to the road surface. In contrast a standard tyre tends to lift the shoulder, hence reducing cornering power and introducing wear (Fig. 17).

As an additional safety feature a sealant has been developed which becomes liquid as the tyre temperature increases following partial deflation. The liquid then acts as a sealant and ensures that no further damage occurs. Tests have proven that this sealing system reduces the incidence of deflation by 3 to 1.

Some run-flat performance has been achieved dependent upon the type of usage to which the tyre is submitted after deflation. It will generally be sufficient to allow the driver to drive the car from a typical motorway deflation situation to the nearest garage off the motorway where the tyre can be replaced. High-speed tyres are not considered repairable after a total deflation; therefore the loss of the tyre by operating it in the run-flat condition until destruction is of no significance.

There were many instances during the substantial endurance programme to which this vehicle was submitted when the bead locking characteristics were thought to have prevented the possibility of serious mishaps following very high-speed deflations.

6 THE ENGINE FAMILY

The primary objectives in designing a new engine for the project were to increase the power output by 10 per cent while reducing the weight by 20 per cent and maintaining the refinement levels for which the current engine is renowned.

From the experience gained on the design of the Coventry Climax F1 engine and on Jaguar racing four-valve V12 engines, it was believed that four-valve configurations offered advantages of power output, torque spread, economy and tolerable emissions. As a result, this technology was chosen for the larger of the engine family (Fig. 18), while the desire to use the existing V12 head line and to introduce an economical and less expensive to build variant for the sub three litre family, dictated a two-valve derivative of the Mayhead.

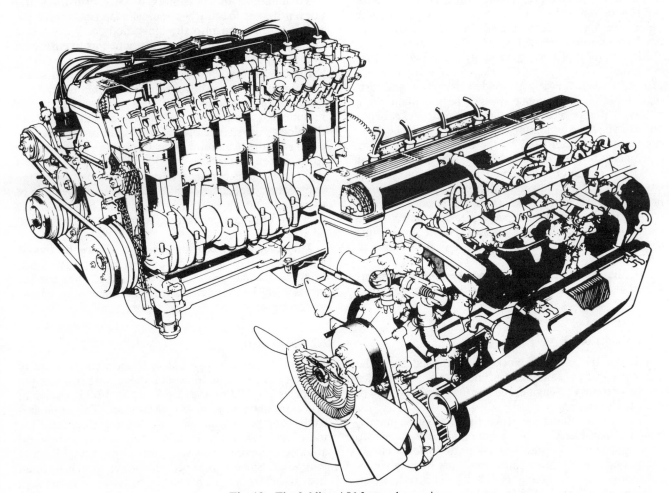

Fig. 18 The 3.6 litre AJ6 four-valve engine

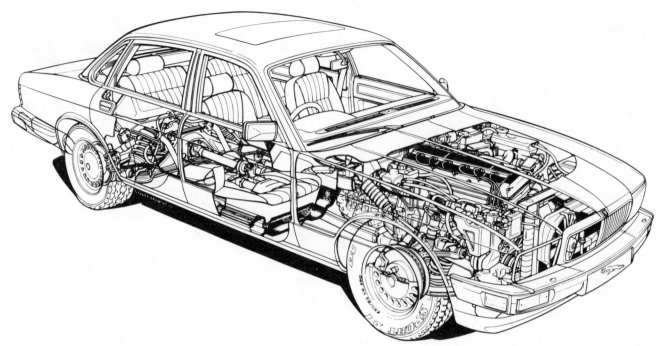

Fig. 19   Cutaway of the XJ40

Other constraints imposed upon the design by the need to utilize existing machinery involved the adoption of bore centre distances of 105 mm and a block main bore diameter of 76.2 mm as used on the V12. Later on in the development programme when volume aspirations increased, a decision was made to create a unique block line, but for reasons described later those principal dimensions remained.

Aluminium had been successfully used for the cylinder block on the V12 engine; therefore, in the interests of weight reduction, it was decided that all major castings for the new engine would be of aluminium, although it was recognized that worldwide experience on six-cylinder aluminium engines was low. The bore centres having been fixed by the desire to use existing machinery, a bore diameter of 91 mm evolved, that being the maximum that could reasonably accommodate good coolant flow. The desire to use an approximately square bore–stroke ratio for good low-speed torque, the optimization of valve size to swept volume and consideration of the overall height limitations determined a 92 mm stroke, giving a swept volume of 3.6 litres.

For the smaller capacity engine the bore was maintained at 91 mm but the stroke was reduced to 75 mm.

6.1 Cylinder block

Originally the cylinder block was designed as a die casting with free standing iron liners, as is the practice on the current V12 engine, and the first prototypes were built to this design.

The cost of tooling for die casting was subsequently, however, considered to be uneconomic for the volumes envisaged and a decision was made to go for a closed deck design, using thin-wall shrink-fit dry liners giving a substantial weight saving of 3.8 kg. The production cylinder block uses LM25 in the fully heat-treated state

with centrifugally cast iron liners, with a wall thickness of 2.3 mm, placed in position when the block has been preheated to a temperature of 180°C, the liners sitting on an abutment at the base of the block.

To minimize the possibility of bore distortion and uneven gasket loading via the cylinder head bolts, the bolts are threaded into the block body well below the cylinder head face and are so positioned as to ensure an even cylinder head gasket loading.

Rigidity of the whole engine and transmission structure was a major consideration and a minimum natural beam-bending frequency of 160 Hz was a design requirement. To achieve this it was necessary to extend the block skirt well below the crankshaft centre-line.

To ease the machining processes, it was an advantage to minimize the width of the block; as a result a separate adapter casting was designed to bolt on to the rear of the cylinder block, also picking up on the base of the aluminium sump, to form an integral rigid assembly to which full diameter transmission bell housings could be attached.

The seven main bearing caps are located by tenons and dowel rings in the cylinder block and are made from nodular cast iron for strength and to minimize the increase in bearing clearance with increasing engine temperature.

6.2 Crankshaft

The crankshaft is supported in seven main bearings of 76.2 mm diameter as indicated above, with a crank pin diameter of 52.98 mm, as used on the 4.2 XK engine in order to maximize facility utilization. The comparatively generous nature of these bearings facilitates the use of nodular cast iron rather than steel. This brought about cost savings and was only 15 per cent less rigid than steel. Since it is 9 per cent lower in density than steel it suffers less of a penalty in terms of crankshaft torsional resonant frequencies.

Secondary benefits exist in that the casting can be made sufficiently accurate to avoid machining the flanks of the webbs, the balance weights being machined on the outer periphery only. The crankshaft employs eight balance weights following the principles established on the XK and V12 engines where the weights are arranged to be effective in a plane perpendicular to that of cylinders 2 and 5, this being the plane in which the greatest centrifugal bending couple is produced by the disposition of the crank pins.

The weights are located either side of crank pins 1, 3, 4 and 6, those adjacent to the inherently heavily loaded centre main bearing, thereby being only 30° displaced from a position directly opposite the corresponding crank pins. The four outer weights are similarly only 30° displaced from the plane of the outer crank pins.

The weight dimensions are such that the couple due to rotating masses is slightly overbalanced, thus obtaining a small relief to the bending in the vertical plane, due to the reciprocating masses. The crankshaft is still, however, some six kilograms lighter than would be the case for a fully counterweighted design.

The crankshaft is nitrocarborized after final grinding and then lapped to ensure that surface deposits left by the hardening process are removed. Positive lip seals are employed at both the front and rear of the crankshaft, these being housed in the timing cover at the front end and in a detachable housing bolted to the cylinder block at the rear. The lip material used in PTFE on a nitrile diaphragm with an additional dust lip seal provided at the front. This was necessary in order to exclude abrasive dust and sand encountered during extensive running in dust-laden Australian conditions.

6.3 Cylinder head assembly

The four-valve cylinder head is an aluminium sand casting in LM25, utilizing a pentroof combustion chamber with the two inlet valves inclined at 24° from the vertical and the two exhaust valves at an angle of 23° from the vertical.

The valves are operated through inverted bucket tappets with adjustment by shimming between the valve stem and the bucket, a practice which has successfully been used on all Jaguar engines since 1949. The tappets run directly in the cylinder head, as is the case on the V12, but are produced from cold formed steel extrusions rather than chilled cast iron as on previous engines in order to reduce the reciprocating masses.

The two overhead camshafts are supported in seven main bearings running directly in the aluminium cylinder head. Inlet valves are made from EN52 and exhaust from 214N. The valve guides are cast iron.

The spark plug is positioned centrally in the chamber to give a fast burn rate and a symmetrical flame front.

The two-valve cylinder head is basically the same as that used on the twelve-cylinder engine, except that outrigger bolts which tie the outside walls of the V12 cylinder block to the cylinder head are no longer necessary with the closed construction of the AJ6 block. The combustion chamber is modified to give the same 12.5 : 1 compression ratio with a larger cylinder displacement and has a slightly deeper squish platform which dictates the use of a shorter inlet valve stem.

6.4 Camshaft and auxiliary drives

A belt drive for the camshaft was seriously considered, but eventually rejected in favour of chain drive for the following reasons.

Firstly, if a single-stage drive to the camshaft is used, a camshaft sprocket twice the diameter of the crankshaft sprocket is required, thereby increasing the overall height of the engine at the point where it is most critical with a sloping bonnet line. Use of a two-stage belt layout was considered but this would have increased the overall length of the engine by approximately 2 inches and this was also unacceptable.

Although belts are now being developed to a stage where they are very reliable, it is still considered that they are not as trouble-free as a chain drive.

Having decided upon a two-stage chain drive it was considered that in order to obtain the most reliable and durable drive for other auxiliaries, such as the power steering pump, they should also be chain driven. As a result, a primary chain drive from the crank also drives an auxiliary shaft at engine speed on the right-hand side of the cylinder block via an intermediate sprocket on the centre-line of the cylinder block. The shaft provides a drive for the PAS pump driven from the rear and a spiral gear to drive the distributor and through the front cover to provide a drive for the power-assisted brake pump.

6.5 Connecting rods and pistons

The connecting rods are of conventional H section forged from manganese steel. The small-end bushes are splash lubricated through drillings in the top of the little end. The bearings are lead bronze with steel backing and are machined to size after pressing into the connecting rod.

Big-end bearings like the mains are lead–bronze and are split steel back shells with a lead–indium overlay. The big-end is split at right angles to the connecting rod and the cap is retained by chrome–molybdenum steel bolts. The rods are balanced and set to a tolerance of ± 2 g. The small ends are also within ± 2 g on any one engine.

The 2.9 litre engine has a connecting rod length 10 mm greater than the 3.6 litre engine to allow for the difference in crankshaft throw between the two engine capacities.

The pistons are cast aluminium alloy with circumferential steel struts to assist in thermal expansion control. The gudgeon pin is made from hardened steel and is fully floating with the end float being controlled by round section circlips. The pin is offset by 1 mm towards the thrust side to eliminate piston rattle. Two compression rings are used, the top being chrome-plated iron, 1.5 mm wide. The second is an iron taper face ring of 2 mm width. The scraper ring is a spring-assisted microland design with chrome-plated running faces.

7 ENGINE MANAGEMENT (7)

Engine management systems are key factors in the attainment of good economy, performance and refinement. Two systems are used in the XJ40, a Bosch system for the 2.9 litre and a Lucas system for the 3.6 litre.

The Lucas system was a new development undertaken for this project, and is therefore the one described here. For precise control it was necessary for the system to be a digitally computed system using a precise method of air mass measurement, taking into account all of the various parameters of water temperature, air temperature, engine load, engine speed, demand etc. To attain the best economy the engine was required to run at the highest practical compression ratio, while maintaining the stringent emission levels required in the United States.

The failed performance had to be of a level considerably better than had been achieved previously and the system had to be capable of a wide range of self-diagnosis. The system that has been developed to achieve all of these aims is a microprocessor-controlled, digital system with mapped ignition, hot wire mass flow anemometry, idle speed control, air injection control and in-built self-diagnostics, with details as follows.

7.1 Airflow measurement

The system chosen was a hot wire anemometry system measuring bypass flow, thus obviating the need for burn-off. The system gives true mass flow and hence takes into account minor variations between engines. It has minimum flow resistance and hence contributes towards optimization of power output. It is highly reliable, having no moving parts, and is capable of extremely rapid response.

7.2 Microprocessor

A digital microprocessor of the capacity type is used to provide accurate data and fast response, while being sufficiently flexible to allow the easy development of market variations. Full feedback control by way of an oxygen sensor is included and the system is adaptive in that it can learn if settings have changed and make adjustments to the memory to compensate.

7.3 Idle speed control

This is a closed-loop control system mounted in the throttle bypass which ensures good low-speed idle, hence improving economy, emissions and refinement and taking into account coolant and ambient air temperatures while compensating for accessory load. This system is also adaptive.

7.4 Supplementary air valve

An extra air valve is included over and above the idle speed control to provide the supplementary air required for operation at sub-zero temperatures.

7.5 Air-injection control

To oxidize unburnt hydrocarbons and carbon monoxide in the manifold during the early part of the cycle and to increase the warm-up rate of the catalyst, an air injection system is used, but only for the brief period

between the coolant temperatures of 15–38°C and below 2500 r/min. Outside these regimes the pump is clutched out to reduce parasitic losses.

7.6 Self-diagnosis

The system is capable of looking at all of the input signals and decides whether these signals are sensible or not. If a failure mode has been detected, it is indicated on the vehicle condition monitor dot matrix at the next start-up and the system reverts to average values which will allow the vehicle to limp home. The failure modes which the system can detect are as follows:

Fault code 1	Spurious crank signal
Fault code 2	Air meter signal open-circuit or earthed
Fault code 3	Water temperature sensor open or short-circuit
Fault code 4	Fuelling feedback system inoperative
Fault code 5	Low throttle pot/high air meter voltages
Fault code 6	High throttle pot/low air meter voltages
Fault code 7	Idle trim, pot short-circuit or 5V
Fault code 8	Air temperature sensor open or short-circuited

8 ELECTRICAL AND ELECTRONIC SYSTEMS (8)

Electrical systems are invariably the most unreliable in any car due to the combination of complexity and the vulnerability to damage while in service and during manufacture. The objective in creating the system for the XJ40 was to double the complexity in response to market requirements but at the same time to improve reliability by an order of five times with a mean failure rate of 1 per cent being demonstrated to a 90+ per cent confidence level.

There are around 200 components and 1.3 km of wire in a new car. The size of the task in testing a system of this complexity against the stated requirements can be judged when one considers that some test batches involved up to 250 components each of which had to pass design lives without failure in order to demonstrate the confidence levels expected.

The main areas of concern on any electrical system centre around the switches, the relays and the connectors, that is all mechanically related components. Electronic components are on the whole very reliable which would normally lead one towards a multiplexed solution. However, multiplexing technology had not developed to the point where it was thought prudent to control the car completely in this manner. Certain multiplexed areas have, however, been introduced for diagnostics and for keyboard operation.

After considerable research, it was decided that a signal wire earth switching technology would be used, as a result of which the area of the wires could be reduced from around 1.0 to 0.5 mm², thus reducing the size of the harnesses considerably. New multi-way connectors up to 0.5 mm were devised with between two and 36-way connections. These are positive-mate anti-backout systems which will either latch or reject upon making and are used for the signal wire connections. In order to cover the power connections which are used in combination with signal connections in areas which needed greater protection, a second level of connector was devised being between two and nine-way and capable of taking 0.5–3 mm connectors. These are also positive-mate anti-backout latch or reject systems, but are capable of being sealed for use in areas where this is demanded.

Relays needed to be developed to an entirely new level of reliability. New specifications were generated which resulted in thousands of units being tested until the desired levels of reliability were achieved. Eventually relays were developed which are an order of magnitude more reliable than those in current use.

Switches required a change in technology from the more normal wiping switch system, which is prone to development of patina and relatively low life, to precious metal switches capable of extremely long lives, operating between -40 and $+85°C$. Switches were developed which, depending upon the power used, are capable of:

$$10 \text{ mA} = 2\,000\,000 \text{ operations}$$
$$250 \text{ mA} = 500\,000 \text{ operations}$$
$$1 \text{ mA} = 150\,000 \text{ operations}$$

Since these switches are very low-movement, low-load devices, it was necessary to incorporate tactile characteristics which would be acceptable to the driver, particularly when operated at night.

To increase the resistance to e.m.c. and e.f.i. a separate logic earth system was used rather than using the vehicle body as a return. To switch the modules, a minimum current of 10 mV is used to avoid any possibility of inadvertent operation due to leakage problems arising with age. The vehicle was developed to have e.m.c. resistance to:

25 V/m on non-critical items
50 V/m on moderately critical items
200 V/m on critical items

to be operative over a range up to 1 GHz.

The result was electrically the cleanest vehicle that we have assessed with the highest back e.m.f. registered for operation of any of the components being -7 V.

To achieve the levels of reliability required, all performance specifications had to be rewritten demanding 100 per cent end of line testing plus burn-in for any logic or microprocessor-based units.

Clearly the size of the development programme was enormous and was far too big for the company to handle alone. To overcome this problem an association was developed with 20 companies in which senior people from each of these companies reported directly to Jaguar during the design and development of the system. Ultimately the programme absorbed 1000 man-years of effort over three years.

The final system encompassed some seven microprocessors driving earthline switching systems for:

Engine management
Air conditioning and heating
Driver information systems
Levelling management
Cruise control
ABS and the central microprocessor

The central microprocessor, in addition to providing overall control, also controls all time-based systems. It is a highly reliable microprocessor with 30 inputs and 30 outputs, having 1 kbyte of ROM, 64 kbytes of RAM and controlling functions from 1 ms to 20 min.

CMOS technology is used throughout in order to reduce quiescent drain which is down to 50 mA. High-quality materials are used throughout, particularly for cables, on which problems were experienced at low temperatures, when the fine cable insulation originally suffered cracking The materials used are HT1 for high-temperature operation, which is capable of enduring temperatures up to 125°C, and HT2 for the more regular operation of up to 105°C.

Cross-polarity and voltage surge protection is provided on all microprocessors and logic units with watchdogging on all microprocessors with reset in the unlikely event of microprocessor crash.

The whole system is protected through a multiple load dump system using zener ring technology.

Features include:

Hot and cold bulb failure detection
Automatic air conditioner operation
Automatic seat heating
Automatic rear screen and mirror operation and timing
Automatic sequence locking of doors, windows and sliding roof
Lighting logic systems

9 POWER SYSTEMS

The XJ40 features a central hydraulic power source which services both the rear suspension self-levelling system and the brake power booster.

Mineral base hydraulic oil is drawn from an under-bonnet reservoir of 1.75 litres capacity by a three-cylinder radial piston pump driven directly from the engine. The pump output passes to a complex valve block containing solenoid-operated valves which direct the oil to either the rear levelling system, the brake system accumulator or back to the reservoir when no system demand activates the unloader circuit. Charging of the brake accumulator takes priority and provides a reserve capability of 0.21 litres at 100 bar, representing an increase in potential energy over a conventional vacuum system of 4.6 times, therefore enhancing the operating reserve of the system in the event of an engine failure.

The service brake system itself is conventional hydrostatic, utilizing normal brake fluid. Actuation is by a tandem master cylinder specially designed to give optimum performance in conjunction with the ABS, and retains the redundant centre seal configuration necessary to minimize the risk of system failure. The foundation brakes themselves are colette-type calipers, that is single-sided 'fist' type, both front and rear, the fronts being 60 mm bore operating on 295 mm diameter by 22 mm thick vented rotors and the rears 36 mm bore operating on 278 mm diameter by 10 mm thick solid rotors. The rear disc also incorporates the drum for the 180 mm diameter drum handbrake, which is cable operated.

The most significant change from earlier systems has

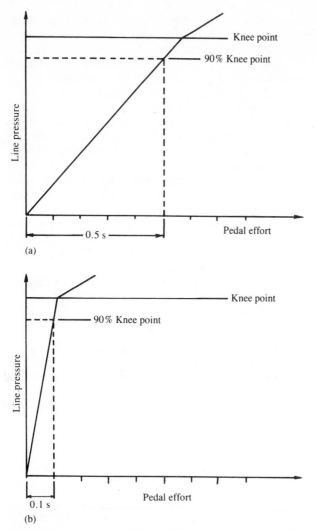

Fig. 20 Power booster performance (a) vacuum and (b) power

method of operation of the company at all levels; not only did the engineering function have to conduct much more strenuous rig and road testing programmes than ever before, but also the supplier body and our own manufacturing processes needed serious review.

There were two fundamental elements in the way this was achieved. The first was the construction of 'component performance standards' designed not just to determine the materials used in the construction of a part and its functional performance levels but also the manner in which the part was to be made and to be maintained at the required reliability and quality levels while in production.

The construction of these performance specifications was an enormous task rivalling the design of the vehicle itself and taking a period of five years to complete. All in all 303 specifications were created.

The second and equally important step was to ensure that agreements were reached between the component suppliers and engineering on all matters related to the performance and reliability of the component. This involved engineering sign-off tests, supplier quality assurance procedures, packaging, line storage, vehicle environment and manufacturing looping processes designed to stop poor quality components being released by the supplier. This was a laborious and painstaking process involving hundreds of suppliers at many thousands of meetings, but it was essential to ensure the achievement and maintenance of the quality levels that were being sought.

11 RIG TEST PROGRAMME

In order to achieve a minimum of 90 per cent confidence level, testing was carried out on up to 250 components which had to complete the test cycle without failure. To do this the design and construction of a large number of dedicated rigs was required. So significant was this programme that it required the setting up of an entirely separate rig design and manufacturing department.

During the course of the programme 94 dedicated rigs were completed ranging from relatively simple to very complex computer driven systems involving in one case the complete environmental cycling of every electrically driven component in the vehicle. The separate assemblies required 340 unique test procedures, which was supplemented by a supplier rig test programme comprising 384 V rigs, many supplied by the rig design and manufacture department.

Over and above these test procedures there was an assurance test programme on off-tool production parts comprising 179 programmes.

Although significant work had been done to improve failure prediction and detection, particularly by the incorporation of road load data techniques (9), it was thought unwise at this stage in the development of the company to abandon road and environmental testing.

An important element in any environmental testing is that the vehicles to be tested are built by the manufacturing process. To this end a dedicated stand-alone assembly line was constructed which was identical in every way to the line that would be built for the final production assembly, upon which all engineering, semi-engineered and fully engineered prototypes would be

been the adoption of a closed centre power booster, which achieves higher and more consistent performance due to the increased knee point; that is the point at which power assistance is exhausted and higher line pressure can only be achieved by considerably increasing the pedal load (Fig. 20a and b), giving a potential stopping distance gain of 14 ft from 60 mile/h at gross vehicle weight, and the presence of the accumulator provides a constant energy source independent of engine speed, load or temperature.

The power booster also considerably improves underbonnet packaging and aesthetics, being a very compact and neat device, a factor which cannot be ignored when underbonnet space is at a premium.

10 TESTING FOR RELIABILITY

The overall objectives of the project were to halve the faults occurring in the first year of warranty when measured against the current vehicle, and to produce a vehicle with 150 000 mile life or twelve years of normal motoring without major component failure.

To achieve this, the majority of the functioning components in the vehicle had to demonstrate a 99 per cent reliability level with a confidence level in excess of 90 per cent. This required a fundamental change in the

built, totalling, by the end of the programme, in excess of 250 vehicles.

Road testing took place in all areas of the world where the vehicle was to be marketed. In Phoenix, Arizona, a new facility was constructed to provide a durability and development base. From there vehicles could be tested in the Arizona Desert or along the mountain passes to the north of Phoenix, offering both extremes of temperature and rates of temperature change. In this area $1\frac{1}{4}$ million miles of testing were completed.

In Timmins, Canada, testing was carried out during the winter months with temperatures down to $-45°C$ being experienced. At this site 1.156 million miles of testing took place.

To the north of Sydney and in Cobar, New South Wales, Australia, 1.783 million miles were accumulated.

In Oman in Muscat, 104 000 miles were added, while in Europe testing was carried out at the Nardo high-speed test track in Italy where 702 000 miles of near flat-out mileage were accumulated and where vehicles were only signed off if they completed 25 000 miles without failure.

At MIRA (Motor Industry Research Association) near Nuneaton, 4200 pavé miles were completed on two vehicles and at the BL test facility at Gaydon, 120 000 miles were successfully completed on the arduous G40 cycle.

United Kingdom mileage totalled 560 000 miles while in the streets of New York two prototypes ran for 79 000 miles. All in all the total road mileage programme accumulated over 5.6 million miles on a total of 89 vehicles. During this period 65 simulated first year warranty periods were assessed, 485 reports were produced and actioned and failure rates well within programme targets were achieved.

12 IMPROVEMENTS IN QUALITY AND PRODUCTIVITY THROUGH IMPROVED MANUFACTURING TECHNIQUES

The objectives set within manufacturing at the start of the project were to double volumes, to double productivity, to double the inventory turn and to halve the faults per car. During the course of the programme the improvements made to the business and its product rendered these targets insufficient, resulting in considerable improvements over and above those original objectives.

The project was tackled on three fronts: quality, productivity and management.

12.1 Quality

From the outset there was the closest possible liaison between manufacturing engineering and product engineering to enable manufacturing aspirations with regard to ease and quality of manufacture to be encapsulated within the original design. Computer aided design (CAD) became a key feature in this development. Manufacturing engineering acquired 30 screens and trained 75 engineers in CAD skills. As a result the manufacture of jigs and fixtures and the integration of the CAD database with computer numerical control (CNC) machining facilities greatly improved the precision and speed with which the associated manufacturing programmes could be achieved.

This is particularly important for the made-in parts. However, improved productivity and quality is not confined to the manufacturing processes but also plays a part in improving the productivity within the technical offices, particularly the output from jig and tool designers and facility and layout engineers.

Capital investment in quality has been substantial, as is evident in all three factories in such areas as:

1. Adaptive weld monitoring devised to monitor critical welding parameters and to ensure weld integrity.
2. An automated bodyside facility leading to a fully integrated but flexible body construction facility.
3. Cathodic electrocoat and clear overbase paint processes for both metallic and solid colours.
4. Advanced transfer lines for heads, blocks and crankshaft machines for the new engine.
5. State-of-the-art engine balancing facilities.
6. Automatic shim selection for tappet clearance.
7. New hot and cold engine test facilities.
8. Advanced testing systems, including rolling roads, using the diagnostic system referred to later in this paper.
9. Statistical process control has been introduced on a wide range of processes, both within Jaguar's manufacturing processes and at suppliers.
10. Additionally, actions have been taken with the whole workforce by the introduction of quality circles, to ensure full commitment to the quality of the product and to harness the enthusiasm of the whole workforce in attaining the quality levels being sought.

12.2 Productivity

As stated earlier, the principal objective was to double productivity. However, during the course of the project the productivity of the business as a whole improved by 2.5 times, thereby rendering the original target obsolete. A more meaningful measurement is to compare the new vehicle productivity with the current vehicle at the time of launch of the new vehicle. The overall effect of the actions described below has been to improve the productivity by that measure by 25 per cent.

First and most important in this process has been the involvement of manufacturing in the design of the vehicle. As a result of the combined effort the design has been affected in the following areas:

1. The adoption of a monoside frame complete but for the rear quarter which is excluded to give flexibility for future model derivatives.
2. The 30 per cent reduction in spot welds.
3. Improved manufacture and simpler assembly techniques, for instance the elimination of any glueing in the trimming process.
4. A design which ensured that body drop assembly could be effected.
5. Additionally, in selected areas, automation and robotics have been applied where the volumes supported their use or where the quality that resulted could not be achieved by conventional means. At launch, around ten robot cells will be working, including:

> bonnet assembly welding and glueing,
> parcel shelf and luggage floor welding,
> crush tube and valance welding,

port polishing,
valve guide and seat insertion,
water pump assembly,
CNC glazing.

The philosophy has been to introduce such systems only as and when they can be justified, and as such the manufacturing process is constantly under scrutiny as volume increases and as the cost of robotics decreases.

12.3 Management

At an early stage it was decided that there would be an overall manager of the project to ensure that the vehicle entered production with as few problems as possible and that the director of the project should report to a member of the company board. This ensured that he was given sufficient authority to push the project through.

A number of policy decisions were made around the project which had significant impact upon its ultimate success. These included:

1. The setting up of a pilot line facility to manufacture all of the fully engineered prototypes for product testing purposes, to construct the early pilot build cars and to act as a training ground for personnel who were later to build the car on the production lines. This eliminated any possibility of disrupting current production schedules by a disorderly introduction of a new product. The pilot line was a complete replica of the production line on which the volume vehicles were to be built.
2. Additionally, a number of control systems were introduced, such as facility monitoring via on-line computer systems, at both the body and engine manufacturing plants, to give a minute by minute status of all production equipment and to provide instant diagnosis of all malfunctions and breakdowns, in order to ensure a rapid maintenance response.
3. Quality monitoring with trackside screens displaying faults identified on the tracks at the body plant.
4. Quality surveillance centres were set up at the vehicle assembly plant to comprehensively audit samples of vehicles and to give the highest possible level of quality assurance.
5. On-line stock recording and work-in-progress control systems were introduced to improve inventory control and throughput and to ensure security of trackside supplies.
6. Vehicle order tracking and control systems were introduced to monitor the progress of customer audit and to ensure that delivery times were achieved to schedule.
7. Labour time and attendance recording systems were introduced to balance schedules and to achieve programme throughput levels.
8. The comprehensive introduction of simulation techniques to validate capacities, process cycle times and control production.

The overall effect of the actions taken has been to improve productivity by a further 25 per cent over the gains already made, raising the productivity from around six to eight cars per manufacturing employee. Work-in-progress and manufacturing inventory levels have been controlled to the point where a better than 20 times inventory turn is being achieved and stocks have been reduced to only three or four days cover.

Further significant steps have been made towards process control and the assurance of the quality levels which the company is seeking.

13 SERVICING THE PRODUCT (10)

The area in which the XJ40 departs from conventional design is in the electrical system described in Sections 6 and 7.

In servicing the electrical system on any automobile two major problems are encountered in electrical failure correction. These are, firstly, the process by which cure is achieved by substitution and, secondly, the problem of 'no fault found' in the returned component, usually because the fault lay in a connection problem or an associated part rather than the part that is returned. 'No fault found' is often a very high percentage of returned parts.

The XJ40 electrical system is far too complex to be handled by this method. Indeed logic-based systems which do not require continuous currents to cause them to operate can often be damaged by unskilled intrusion. It was apparent, therefore, very early on in the programme that an entirely new method of servicing would have to be designed in parallel with the development of the vehicle electrical system.

What was needed was a computer-based system which could easily be updated in line with model year changes, and was operator friendly, using visual displays for prompting and readout. The system had to be stand-alone since world networks are not available in many areas in which the vehicle is to be marketed, but had to be readily adaptable for the time when this was possible. The system had to have a failure recording system for inclusion with returned parts, it had to be compatible with production line systems and had to be programmed in a number of languages to suit the company's marketing needs.

The system finally chosen was a Genrad product, which is a robust reliable system incorporating the following features and designated the Jaguar Diagnostic System:

1. It is designed to be capable of interfacing to an exceptionally wide range of test subjects and has a flexible input and output design.
2. It was originally developed as a portable test system and is rugged in construction and able to tolerate an unusually wide range of environmental conditions.
3. As a runtime test system it is designed for dynamic testing and control of digital logic-based equipment.
4. Its software architecture is purpose designed to allow optimum implementation of automated test programmes in a user friendly way.
5. The system design offers suitable opportunities for future enhancement to cater for alternative vehicle electronic technologies and communications etc.
6. The supplying company was able to offer worldwide field support through its network of service locations.
7. Ease of software update ability for the end user.
8. Flexible screen display.

The system itself comprises a 2610-based system processor with:

Z80A microprocessor (4 MHz clock)
512K RAM
5 in CRT display
double-sided double density disc drive
800K formatted storage
video output for an additional monitor
RF232 serial communication port
battery-backed real-time clock
four-card expansion port

Development of the system was a co-operative venture involving Jaguar, Genrad and Cirrus and involved five years of development.

The result is possibly the most sophisticated diagnostic system available anywhere in the motor industry. It is capable of rapid updating and is operable by relatively unskilled personnel. The same system is used in the manufacturing process for fault diagnosis, it is immediately updatable worldwide, and provides the customer with a fast accurate service at minimum cost. It has eliminated cure by substitution and the 'no fault found' problem.

14 TRAINING

During the design and development of the new vehicle there was a continuing need for well-qualified and experienced engineers to meet the expanding needs of the programme. The skills required were wide and various, including expertise in electronics and microprocessors, vehicle and engine management systems, computer aided design and computer aided manufacture, finite element analyses, geometric modelling, road load data analysis, ergonomics, noise and vibration, aerodynamics and body design skills.

In a large number of areas it was apparent very early in the programme that the skills that were required were not readily available and as a result it became necessary to train in-house to support the programme.

Specific courses were set up in electronics, body and mechanical engineering, computer aided design and body design. External courses were used at such institutions as Hatfield Polytechnic for body design, Loughborough University for electrical design and ergonomics, and Lanchester Polytechnic, Coventry, for design, noise vibration and aerodynamics, added to which there were specific turnkey teaching systems acquired for road load data, finite element analysis and NASTRAN.

Higher education was supported in a number of areas including MSc courses in computer aided engineering at Aston University.

The company has invested very heavily in CAD during the programme such that at the time of writing there are 90 terminals within product and manufacturing engineering with plans to double those numbers in the next few years. This involved the training of 320 engineers to various levels of CAD expertise, amounting to 1570 training days. The shortage of body engineers involved the development of a conversion course which is an intensive six months in-house course, designed to take people from a wide range of skills and convert them into body designers. In two years 30 engineers were ultimately placed in the design area by this means.

The introduction of modern technology into manufacturing areas dictated the need to retrain first-line supervisors, operators, craftsmen and manufacturing engineers to ensure that they had the ability to control and maintain the required production and quality levels. These needs were progressively met over a period of three years, again through programmes run by the company and supported by major suppliers of equipment and component parts. In all, some 3500 employees received training in robotics and CNC applications, paint and main assembly processes.

The pilot facility mentioned earlier was established, not only to manufacture prototypes and pilot build cars but also to prove manufacturing processes and give operators and supervisors experience prior to moving on to the main assembly tracks.

Planning has not only been confined to the in-house needs of the company but has also been extended to the dealer network. The training has concentrated on the introduction of vehicle electronics and a comprehensive programme of sales and service training covering all aspects of the vehicle in every market.

In the UK alone some 560 dealer staff will have been trained by the time the vehicle is launched.

A training programme for European and overseas dealer staff is also underway and will be completed before overseas launch of the vehicle.

An extensive dealer training video programme was developed involving substantial investment in hardware and software to provide a uniform level of skill throughout the entire market place. An indication of the level of commitment by the company to training the workforce can be gained by reference to the training days used.

In 1985 a total of 38 300 training days were committed, that is four days per average employee, while in 1986 the number of training days planned is 46 300—a rise to 4.5 days per average employee.

15 CONCLUSIONS

The first objective in the production of any new automobile is to satisfy the customer. The luxury sector places very special demands upon the product and as a result there are some very fine motor cars available. The company's need was to offer a viable alternative in its character, offering status and beauty with new levels of quality, reliability and service, coupled to improved performance in all aspects. To create this product the company had to tread a careful path between innovation and tradition.

To achieve these aims the project has involved the development of a number of new technologies and the application of innovative management techniques, in order to solve the resource problems associated with a company which, at the start of the project, was close to extinction.

The processes used during the development have been a mixture of new and tried and trusted methods which were brought to bear as the development of the company grew alongside the development of the project.

The result is a project which is seen by observers as a logical development of the Jaguar tradition. It has features attractive to a larger buying group than has been hitherto the case without disenchanting traditional customers. With this vehicle it will have been demonstrated that the company is capable of regenerating its product and is set for further logical developments from this base.

REFERENCES

1 **Fowler, R. J.** Development of an in-car climatic control system. *Proc. Instn Mech. Engrs*, Part D, 1986, **200**, this issue.
2 **Holtum, C.** The design and assessment of the Jaguar XJ40 instruments and controls. *Proc. Instn Mech. Engrs*, Part D, 1986, **200**, this issue.
3 **Arrowsmith, M. J.** The design and development of the XJ40 seating system. *Proc. Instn Mech. Engrs*, Part D, 1986, **200**, this issue.
4 **Brown, A. M.** and **Dunn, J. W.** A dynamic modelling technique for the XJ40 body structure design. *Proc. Instn Mech. Engrs*, Part D, 1986, **200**, this issue.
5 **Cartwright, A. J.** The development of a high comfort, high stability rear suspension. *Proc. Instn Mech. Engrs*, Part D, 1986, **200**, this issue.
6 **Day, P. S., Holmes, T.** and **Major, D. J.** TD tyres for Jaguar. *Proc. Instn Mech. Engrs*, Part D, 1986, **200**, this issue.
7 **Baxendale, A. E.** Development of an air mass flow sensing microprocessor-based fuelling and ignition system for the Jaguar XJ40. *Proc. Instn Mech. Engrs*, Part D, 1986, **200**, this issue.
8 **Haslett, R. A.** and **Scholes, P. J.** A vehicle electrical system from concept to production. *Proc. Instn Mech. Engrs*, Part D, 1986, **200**, this issue.
9 **Tivey, C.** The utilization of fatigue life prediction techniques in support of a major vehicle project. *Proc. Instn Mech. Engrs*, Part D, 1986, **200**, this issue.
10 **Andrews, M. J.** Development of a service support system for microprocessor-controlled vehicle electrical systems. *Proc. Instn Mech. Engrs*, Part D, 1986, **200**, this issue.

A vehicle electrical system from concept to production

R A Haslett, BSc, PhD and P J Scholes
Jaguar Cars Limited, Coventry

This paper describes the features of the electrical system for the XJ40 Jaguar car, and the testing methods used to prove the reliability of the design. The system includes a number of engineering changes which are novel to the automotive industry.

1 INTRODUCTION

The new car was conceived to replace the existing Jaguar saloon in the same market sector. The main characteristic of a classic style, reflecting British workmanship and taste, was to be retained. However, competitor cars were already incorporating an increasing number of features for the occupants, which the purchaser would expect. In the wake of these features was an inevitable greater engineering complexity. Nevertheless, it was decided that these features must be included, and the car was to achieve a lower incident of component failures than had previously been demonstrated in passenger cars.

These triple goals of classic style, extensive electrical features for the car and a new standard in the reliability of every component presented a unique engineering challenge. The goals were met by re-engineering all the electromechanical automotive components which have traditionally given problems and by harnessing electronics technology.

2 APPROACH

A numerical target was specified for the mean tolerable failure rate of the new car electrical system. Failure rates for some similar components were available from current car models. An inspection of the data and a simple mathematical model of the reliability of the total system led to the following conclusions:

1. The achilles heel of the last generation of car electrical systems were connectors, relays and switches. Mean failure rates of these components had to be reduced by a factor of at least four. This led to a fundamental change in the design philosophy of the switches and connectors. The reliability of the devices which were operated by the switching elements such as motors, solenoids and lamps had to be maintained at a level comparable with the best that the worldwide component supplier industry could achieve.
2. More sophisticated vehicle features for the car occupants were only possible by using electronic control modules. These logic modules had to continue to operate for the twelve year life of the car, with a mean failure rate below 1 per cent in the critical first year of life.

Before committing this electrical system to production, a further specification was set: that the reliability targets described above should be demonstrated by experiment, so that the confidence in the final result was better than 90 per cent. This was the most far-reaching directive of all. Eighty-five vehicles were driven in the earth's harshest environments for distances of 50 000–150 000 miles.

Millions of pounds were invested in new test equipment such that batches of up to 250 component samples could be exposed to simulated life tests under laboratory conditions to search out the common and uncommon modes of failure.

3 DESIGN

3.1 Principles

An initial cursory examination of the total electrical system revealed that there were about 200 components and that the interlinking signal and power cables could cause congestion in the bulkhead, behind the instrumentation and facia. Multiplexing of signal wires was rejected at that time, as the components suppliers were unwilling to undertake such a radical redesign of their products. Cable congestion was relieved by reducing signal cable sizes from 1.0 to 0.5 mm^2. A new compact multi-way connector was designed, with a pin diameter of 1.5 mm, fitted in plastic mouldings which housed 15, 24 and 36 pins. The housings have a number of features largely new to the automotive environment, which include a plate to prevent back-out of the crimped terminal and a latch and ramp arrangement which ejects the plug if it is not fully located in its mating socket (Fig. 1).

A larger connector to accommodate pins carrying higher current was also produced, following the same design principles.

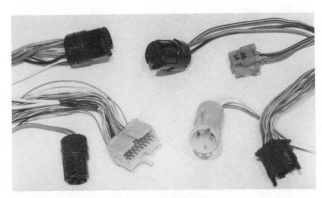

Fig. 1 Connectors

0265-1904/86 $2.00 + .05

In general, the return path for electric current flow in passenger cars is taken through the body metalwork. High instantaneous currents for power-consuming motors and heaters can cause significant voltage differences through the body, which may affect the logic switching levels in electronic modules. Therefore, a separate earth logic circuit was created running through the wiring harness, such that all logic circuits could be referenced to the battery negative terminal, isolating any interference from power-consuming devices.

It was also speculated that intermittent faults could be caused by radiofrequency interference induced on the signals in the wiring harness. To minimize circuit impedance and sensitivity, the minimum current flow in any circuit incorporated in the harness was set at 10 mA.

Conventional switches, based on base metal contacts, are a common source of failure (1). In the design of this car, the switches were acting as inputs to a microprocessor, so they were only required to carry a low current, and a new approach was valid. Switch elements were formed from a domed metal foil on top of a contact on a printed circuit board (Fig. 2). The surfaces were plated with precious metals and sealed from the environment by an adhesive membrane to prevent contact degradation. The dome was then pressed against the printed circuit board by a mechanism actuated by the driver. The deflection characteristics of the domed clicker plate provided a tactile feel.

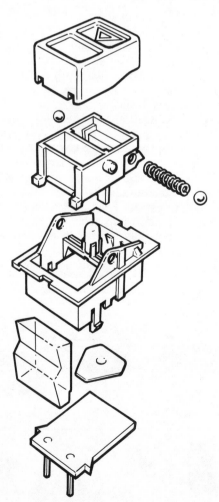

Fig. 2   Sketch of exploded switch

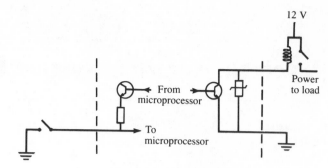

Fig. 3   Logic switches

Many of the vehicle functions controlled directly by the driver were operated through a microprocessor. In this way, an output could be actuated from a logical decision based on two or more inputs, which may be from either momentary action or latched switches (see Fig. 3). The control unit could also perform time delays. One example is that the interior light is turned on by opening the driver's door and will remain on for 15 seconds after the door closes if the seat is occupied, but will turn off immediately if the seat is unoccupied or the ignition is turned on.

In many cases, the transistor output signals of the vehicle control units were amplified through relays to deliver sufficient current for the various lamps and motors. A philosophy of earth line switching of the relay coils was adopted, to simplify the transistor circuit arrangement within the control unit.

3.2 Central timing unit

These general principles led to the circuit arrangement shown in Fig. 4, for the timing unit which operates many of the comfort and convenience features for the driver. This unit controls indicator flash rate, heated seats and rear window, a windscreen and headlamp washer system and the windscreen wiper. A central locking switch will lock all doors and the boot, and raise the electric windows in sequence. The state of each of the input switches to the microprocessor is measured each 16 ms, using a polling system which energizes each switch with a 5 V pulse and senses if current flows.

Since some of the functions of this control unit, such as the interior light, operate before the ignition is turned on, it is permanently powered from the battery.

3.3 Instrumentation

The instrument cluster presented a particularly difficult styling decision (2), since a large amount of information had to be displayed while retaining a pleasing appearance. Two circular moving coil meters were chosen for the speedometer and tachometer and a vacuum fluorescent dot matrix (32 × 32) for the eleven types of warning signals emanating from different control units and sensors on the car (Fig. 5). Below the matrix are two lines of 20 characters, which may either describe an ISO warning symbol or present information on the journey or fuel consumption. The trip computer is operated by nine keys to give nine possible items of display information and the facility to input the intended

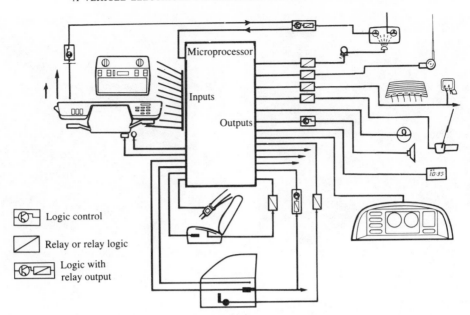

Fig. 4 Microprocessor for timing functions

journey length (**2**). The fuel quantity in the tank, the oil pressure, cooling temperature and battery voltage are presented as bar graphs in vacuum fluorescent technology. The odometer is in the same display technology, the information being held and updated in **EPROM** within the panel. The instrument panel is driven by electronic signals, including the speed signal originating from a variable reluctance sensor, excited by a toothed wheel on the rear axle assembly (Fig. 6).

3.4 Engine management

There are two six-cylinder engine variants for the car, of 3.6 litre and 2.9 litre. Fuel is introduced by timed intake port injection, and the engine management systems control both fuel and ignition timing. The primary sensors are air mass flow and engine speed. The airflow sensors are of the heated wire type, although the version on the 2.9 litre is exposed to the full airflow, while the other in the 3.6 litre is of a flow bypass arrangement. A toothed wheel on the crankshaft behind the pulley excites a sensor to generate an engine speed signal and a missing tooth on that wheel indicates the crankshaft position.

Secondary analogue sensors detect cooling temperature and throttle position. The engine control unit for the 3.6 litre engine has the facility to detect certain engine sensor failures. A serial diagnostic data link informs the microcomputer in the instrumentation panel, where the fault code is displayed for the driver on the dot matrix display, and the engine control unit assumes a limp-home mode.

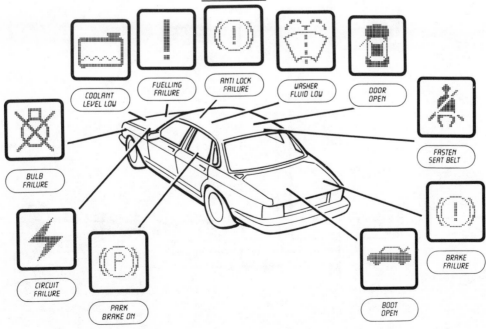

Fig. 5 Instrumentation warning symbols

Fig. 6   Instrument panel

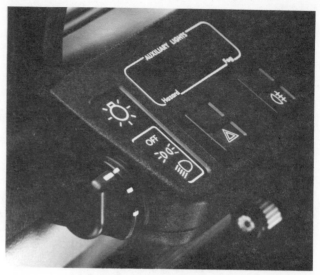

Fig. 7   Lighting switch

3.5 Lighting control

The switches which control the exterior lamps (Fig. 7) are also of the low-current form, acting as signals to a circuit in the facia panel. The logic circuit prevents the selection of certain combinations of lamps, prohibited by legislation. The outputs from the lighting logic circuit energize relays located within modules at the four corners of the vehicle. The relays, in turn, provide current to the adjacent lamps. The four relay modules also contain electronic circuits which can detect current flow to the bulbs and will locate a failed bulb whether it is illuminated or not, provided the ignition is turned on (**3**). Outputs from the four modules are arranged in a 'wired OR' configuration, and will activate bulb failure warning signals on the dot matrix display of the instrument panel (Fig. 8).

The universal turn indicator has been replaced by an electronic version, where the steering column stalk switch does not latch but is only momentarily depressed by the driver and returns to the central position. The low-current switch signal activates the central timing processor and the appropriate lamps are operated through the relay modules. The microprocessor cancels the turn indicator by sensing the position of a magnet on the steering column with three reed relays.

3.6 Comfort control

A new air conditioning unit was designed for this car, based on a system of two rotary flaps to control the mixing of hot and cold air. The flaps are operated by servo motors and feedback potentiometers linked to a microprocessor. The driver can select the range and distribution of temperature and humidity conditions

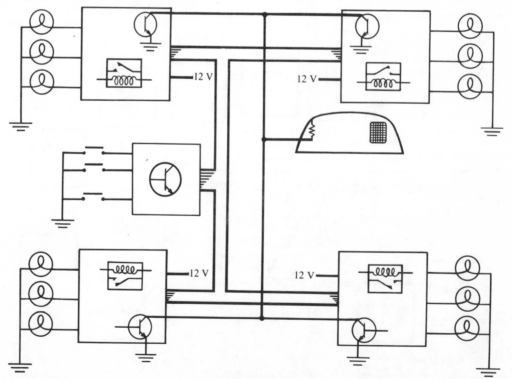

Fig. 8   Lighting and bulb failure circuit

within the vehicle using the control panel on the centre console. The last conditions selected are retained while the ignition is turned off. The temperature within the car, and of the induced air, is measured by active semi-conductor sensors, which yield a voltage proportional to absolute temperature. A complete description of the system is contained in reference (4).

3.7 Anti-skid

A proprietary anti-lock braking system was chosen, where the speed of each of the four wheels is detected by a variable reluctance sensor and toothed wheel. These signals are produced by a control unit which in turn actuates valves to modify the braking pressure on the wheels and prevent wheel locking and yaw of the vehicle during braking manoeuvres (5).

3.8 In-car entertainment

A number of commercial radio receivers were assessed against the performance specification of a good dynamic range and minimum distortion. For the high-line model car, an electronic tuned unit with an auto-reverse cassette was chosen. The speakers within the passenger compartment are arranged with two base speakers in the heel board below the rear seat and four treble speakers within the arm rests. This gives excellent sound reproduction, the heel board acting as a horn to give balance to the low-frequency components.

3.9 Battery alternator

This complex electrical system places a heavy load on the battery and alternator. By careful component choice, the quiescent current drain from the battery is kept below 50 mA with the ignition off. By removing certain fuses during shipping, this can be reduced by a further 25 mA. This is sufficient to allow the vehicle to be started on arrival at the port of entry of each market.

In cold climates at night, all heating features and the lights consume over 100 A for a period of a few minutes. To check that the alternator and battery have adequate capacity to start the engine, suburban and city driving cycle tests were conducted in extreme hot and cold climates. Many of the heater elements are under the control of the timing microprocessor, so their active time period is defined by the design. These experiments illustrated that an alternator with a maximum output of 80 A could not supply the demand, and that an output of at least 90 A was necessary.

4 RELIABILITY

A component fitted to a car must endure a wide range of environmental and operating conditions. The process of proving that the component design is adequate is defined in the component test specification. One of the initial problems faced by the design team was that all existing component test specifications referred to conventional electromechanical automotive systems and had limited relevance to the extensive electronics in this car. Therefore, all component test specifications were totally rewritten (6). The following guidelines were adopted:

1. Eleven general areas of the car were designated, such as the passenger compartment, in contact with the engine, within the engine bay, under the car, on the suspension etc. The location of the component defined its ambient operating temperature and humidity range, whether it was exposed to salt spray and water splash, the maximum vibration level etc.
2. In association with the total system reliability model mentioned previously, ten categories of 'demonstrated reliability' were designated. The particular category into which each component was placed was determined by the repercussions of a total failure of that module on the safety of the vehicle, the likelihood of detection by the driver and the cost of replacement.

The numerical values of the extreme environmental conditions which were simulated by the test procedures were measured in a series of overseas tests on experimental cars in Australia, America, Canada and the Middle East. Between one and five samples of each component was subjected to one or more of these simulated extreme situations in the laboratory, using IEC and BS test procedures. Endurance tests were devised to demonstrate that the component would achieve the reliability targets for the life of the car. Where the electrical component contains mechanical moving parts such as a switch, motor or solenoid, the number of operations, during a typical twelve year life were estimated. An automated mechanism or rig was then designed for each component, so that the operations could be carried out continuously, to accelerate the life cycle and induce any latent failure modes. A typical rig for endurance testing of steering column switches controlled and monitored by a programmable logic controller is shown in Fig. 9.

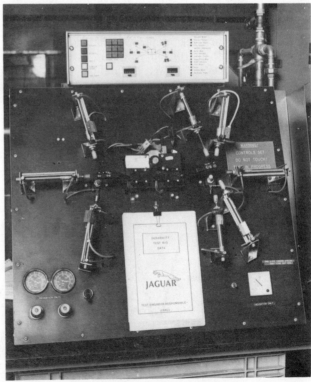

Fig. 9 Steering column switchgear

Different methods are available for accelerating the life cycle of components containing electronic elements, such as transistors and integrated circuits. The silicon junction can be stressed by increasing the operating temperature. The relationship between the probability of failure of each junction at normal operating temperature and the elevated test temperature is estimated by the Arrhenius equation (7). For example, if a normal component ambient temperature of 30°C is raised to 85°C the probability of failure is increased by a factor of 20. Thus, where a component is powered only when the ignition is on, a typical 5000 hour operating life can be condensed to 250 hours at the elevated temperature. Bonded and soldered joints within chips or on printed circuit boards often receive their maximum stresses during thermal shock conditions, due to differing thermal capacities and rates of expansion.

Therefore, any test regime which will accelerate the life of an electronics sub-assembly must contain the elements of high temperature and high rate of temperature change. The thermal cycle shown in Fig. 10 was chosen based on these considerations.

During the test, the ignition battery supplies were connected during one half of the cycle, and all solid state outputs were cycled through typical operating conditions. Thus, the thermal cabinets within which the components were tested also contained wiring looms to connect with realistic loads mounted outside the chamber; engine management control units were connected to injectors, central timing units to relay coils, bulbs and motors, and cruise control units to pumps and solenoid valves etc.

The number of samples of each component which were required to pass the durability test were calculated based on the reliability targets, using binomial probability tables. For example, the reliability target for the instrument cluster and other complex electronic assemblies was 99 per cent, to be demonstrated with a 92 per cent confidence. This meant that 250 samples had to survive the 35 day temperature cycle without impairment of their operating characteristics (8).

A batch of 50 instrument panels in a test chamber, with the associated power, excitation and loading equipment, is illustrated in Fig. 11. In addition to this programme of component simulation tests, experimental vehicles were driven for 100 000 miles through the winter in Canada, at ambient temperatures below −30°C, and in Australia at temperatures above 40°C. Test cars were also placed in a radiation test chamber to identify any malfunction associated with radio inter-

Fig. 11   MEL test chamber

ference in the band of 20 mHz to 1 GHz at an amplitude of 50 V/m. These tests continued over a period of three years, identifying problems and making improvements on subsequent experimental cars.

This enormous programme revealed numerous design faults. For example, during endurance tests many switches stopped functioning early in their life cycle, custom logic chips failed during thermal cycling, internal component connectors became open circuit and relay contacts seized. In the vehicle tests, cable insulation cracked at low temperatures, sealed connectors and lamps leaked and corroded, radiofrequency interference at low signal strengths caused dangerous fault conditions etc.

Components went through the process of design, test and redesign up to four times before the required reliability was demonstrated and they were accepted for production. In turn, the production processes were organized to maintain the standards of reliability and quality which had been achieved on the prototype sample. However, the mechanisms employed are not described in this paper.

5 PROJECT MANAGEMENT

The design and development of the electrical system for this car involved 20 companies, employing a total in the order of 1000 man-years. The co-ordination and management of the project was only possible by imposing strict disciplines and procedures. The most important were:

1. The concept and functional performance of the system and its sub-assemblies were defined by the design team *before* prototype components were made

Input and output currents to simulate vehicle

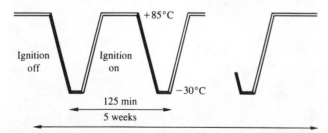

Design validation: 250 samples   In-process validation, 1 sample/week

Fig. 10   Durability test on microprocessor and logic modules

or placed in experimental vehicles. Similarly, the authority to change any component based on test failures or aesthetic considerations remained with the design team.

2. Senior representatives of all companies who supplied major components attended a regular meeting to ensure that the policies were applied consistently and the progress of any one company remained in phase with the others.

3. In addition, there were regular technical meetings with each company. A series of stages in the product evolution were defined where the customer and supplier signed a document of agreement that all outstanding anomalies had been resolved. These stages were the completion of the design drawing, the final component installation in the car, final test results to the specification and acceptance of the production process to maintain the standards set for the prototype design.

6 CONCLUSIONS

1. Market requirements for the car dictated a large number of sophisticated features for the occupants, without compromising its classic personality. These were met by combining the elements of conventional automotive electrical systems with electronics technology.

2. High standards of component and system reliability caused radical design revisions and the implementation of new rigorous testing procedures to demonstrate conformance to those standards.

3. The efforts of many engineers in different companies and countries were co-ordinated by a hierarchical system of meetings.

REFERENCES

1 **Embrey, D., Webb, S. F.** and **Legg, G. J.** A non multiplexed microprocessor display driver interface switching system for automotive application. IEE Conf. on *Automotive Electronics*, November 1983, p. 146.

2 **Galer, M., Spicer, J.** and **Holtum, C.** The design and evaluation of a trip computer and a vehicle condition monitor display. IEE Conf. on *Automotive Electronics*, November 1983, p. 192.

3 **Legg, G. J.** and **Webb, S. F.** Automotive lamp integrity checking systems. IEE Conf. on *Automotive Electronics*, November 1983, p. 171.

4 **Thoburn, R. J.** and **Probert, N. D.** Development for a microprocessor based climate control system for automotive applications. IEE Conf. on *Automotive Electronics*, November 1983, p. 182.

5 **Lieber, H.** and **Czinczel, A.** Four years of experience with 4-wheel antiskid brake systems (ABS). SAE paper 830481.

6 **Sykes, K.** and **Goss, D. J.** *Jaguar electrical component standard*, Issue 3, 1985.

7 *Fairchild Linear Division Reliability Report*, January 1984.

8 **McConachie, E. I.** *BL Technology Reliability Manual*, 1984 (BL Technology Limited, Lighthorne, Warwickshire).

Development of an in-car climatic control system

R J Fowler
Jaguar Cars Limited, Coventry

This paper describes in detail the original methods used in the design and development of a microprocessor-based climate control system for the XJ40 Jaguar car. It takes the concept of air conditioning and applies modern technology and materials to produce a unit for a new passenger car. It describes those areas of design where experience in automotive air conditioning has shown the need for improvement, and also explains the operational procedures. The theories presented can be used in any automotive application and lead through concept and development to a final design implementation.

1 INTRODUCTION

A new vehicle in today's competitive environment must meet the most stringent performance standards on reliability and performance. This is easily measured for speed and weight and the other, oft-quoted parameters, but it must also compete in areas where regular measurements fail to grasp the overall effects. The climatic environment, the living space, the comfort in which a driver is maintained enhances not only safety but also the perceived performance of the total vehicle. Any changes in the interior climate may drastically affect the vehicle user to an extent where the user is physically uncomfortable.

To achieve Jaguar objectives on the XJ40 meant a complete redesign of the in-car climate control system to incorporate new technology, improved performance and increased reliability.

2 CUSTOMER REQUIREMENTS

Before embarking on a blind redesign of a climate control system, it was necessary to establish the users' requirements. What the customer expected from a system was quite obviously of paramount importance.

To this end a series of programmes were started involving ergonomics, competitor surveys, customer surveys and, of course, a close examination of the physiological requirements of the human body.

Many factors were assessed for both understanding and necessity—whether outlets should be warm or cool, what level of airflow was acceptable—and every feature had to be considered for all world markets. This meant wide-ranging ambient conditions from sub-zero arctic conditions to extreme desert situations, from night to high radiant sunlight and from torrential rain to arid drought. Each change in environment must be crossed with no change to the vehicle user and to do this in a controlled manner was the prime consideration. From the investigations into customer requirements a set of ideal conditions were formulated; these were to be achieved by the climate control system which could alter the three main variables:

Temperature
Airflow
Humidity

The surveys also specified low noise as an additional requirement: therefore the task was to meet the needs of temperature and airflow as quietly as possible. Failure in any one specific area could mean dissatisfaction for the user.

3 OBJECTIVES

From the customers came a clear requirement for performance and reliability which complemented the company targets for the new vehicle to form the major objectives:

(a) improved performance over current cars and potential competitors,
(b) increased reliability over potential competitors.

Added to these were a series of company objectives:

(a) reduced weight over current cars,
(b) maintain or reduce existing package size.

These were the main objectives from which the new design would germinate.

4 SPECIFICATION

Having defined the objectives it was necessary to describe the final unit in engineering terms—the specification. This was the far-reaching document which covered all areas of the unit's performance, quality, reliability, weight and noise which would be capable of meeting the company's objectives and hence the customer's requirements.

Every attempt was made in the preparation of this document to prevent the avoidable error and to stop self-interpretation of the company's aims.

This unit was one of the first major systems to carry a full design and process failure mode effects analysis procedure. It took many months to prepare and traced any potential problem and worried it to a satisfactory solution.

A number of suppliers were then issued with this document from which feasibility studies were prepared; a final selection of supplier was then made.

5 THE UNIT

The final design can, in simple terms, be described as a flap-controlled air distribution system. Figure 1 is a cross-section schematic of the main unit, from which it

  0265-1904/86 $2.00 + .05

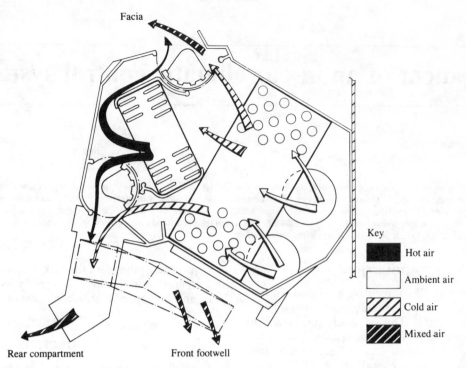

Facia

Key

Hot air

Ambient air

Cold air

Mixed air

Rear compartment   Front footwell

Fig. 1   Schematic of unit

can be seen that air is diverted by two rotary air valves through the heater matrix. This air is proportional to the position of each flap and its relationship to the other.

The main components are held in a three-part plastic case with access for all electrical and mechanical services (Fig. 2). Air is initially routed through an evaporator where it is cooled and dried and is then either warmed or passed directly to the distribution system for dispersion in the car.

Air pressure is generated from two separate blowers, one on either side of the unit, again housed in plastic cases with independent flap and speed control.

The total package is controlled via an electric switch pack mounted in the centre console. From this panel, which is the only visible part of the unit, the user may select any of the variables.

The control brain which interprets the required signals from the unit and user is the microprocessor. This is housed on the side of the main unit and is an 8 bit device developed from a one-chip microcomputer, the 3870. Its shape has been governed by installation constraints and is not of any significance. Specific demands on the microprocessor are made by the user

via the control panel, by the unit via positional sensors and by the climatic conditions via a number of measurement sensors. The processor will analyse the various input signals and make a decision for change, if required, which is output to the unit. At this point the rotary air valves would alter position, thereby changing the in-car condition. A complete system is therefore a closed loop with various measurement devices correcting unit output to maintain the user setting.

6 COMPONENTS, THEIR FUNCTION AND DESIGN

The case for the complete unit is designed in three parts, a rear half to house the evaporator and two front sections holding the heater matrix and rotary air valves. The case (Fig. 3) is a talc-filled polypropylene injection moulding, the material being chosen for its good thermal properties, light weight and strength. The split of the case was designed to avoid possible leak paths for the evaporative condensate and to enable assembly of the moving parts.

Inside the main case are the two rotary air valves

Fig. 2   Main components

Fig. 3   Unit case

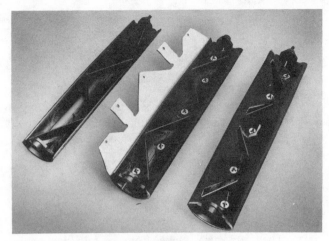

Fig. 4 Rotary air valve

(Fig. 4). These are glass-filled nylon to ensure torsional rigidity as the driving force would be at one end of the central shaft. The sealing edges for these flaps are achieved with a nylon material which wipes across rigid sections of the main case mouldings.

The two main components of the system are also housed within the case assembly: these are the heater matrix (Fig. 5) and an evaporator. The heater matrix is a copper–brass radiator with microfoil fins of very close spacing for performance. The performance was derived using the Series III saloon as a base. Body conductance was measured at various speeds and a straight line prediction made for the working speeds of the vehicle in −30°C ambients.

The graph in Fig. 6 shows vehicle speed against body conductance in watts per kelvin and shows speed limits for Canada and northern Europe where −30°C ambients can be expected. Also shown is the measured miscellaneous heat pick-up from engine and exhaust systems and an overlay of the heater matrix output in kilowatts.

From this is can be found that with an ambient of −30°C and a temperature demand of 24°C the unit must generate 3.58 kW to overcome general heat loss. Additional heat must be generated to increase interior temperature. The specification requires 95 W/K which at 55 miles/h generates 9.88 kW, thereby giving 6.3 kW interior heat. This target was achieved as proven in climatic chamber tests where air outlet temperatures are 46°C average, equating well with calculated data (see Fig. 6).

The matrix is a split unit with removable inlet and

outlet pipes. This, coupled with detachable side plates to the actual unit case, means it is easily serviced in the car without removing the main system. Located on the inlet pipe to the matrix is an electrical temperature switch used for isolation of the systems blowers until a satisfactory water temperature is available. This prevents cold air being drawn into the car during warm-up conditions.

The evaporator (Fig. 7) is a copper tube aluminium fin unit. The fins possess a crinkle appearance to aid water dispersion, thereby maintaining thermal performance during operation. The required evaporative performance was calculated using a maximum world ambient of 52°C with 900 W/m² solar load. To maintain an average interior temperature of 24°C the evaporator must input 4.5 kW to overcome body conductance, driver plus one passenger, miscellaneous heat and solar load.

With the unit under full load it requires an outlet temperature of approximately 4°C to maintain an interior average of 24°C; this equates to 7.39 kW. Using both input criteria means that a total of 11.89 kW is required to maintain the initial objective.

The target specification was, however, set at 8 kW, because full cooling capacity is generated on recirculat-

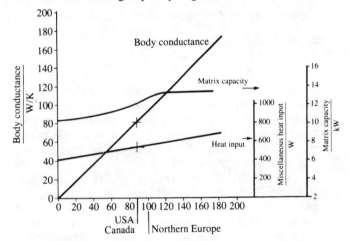

Assumptions

Set speed	55 mile/h
Miscellaneous heat input	0.5 kW
Heat loss, body conductance	4.32 kW
Heat input from driver and one passenger	0.24 kW
Ambient temperature	−30°C
Average interior temperture	24°C
Total heat loss to maintain 24°C interior at 55 mile/h in a −30°C ambient	3.58 kW
Capacity of heater matrix in a −30°C ambient with a 74°C coolant temperature	9.88 kW
Total capacity left to heat interior	6.3 kW

Target performance

1.25 kW per person installed
95 W/K at 88°C, water flow 0.15 L/s, air flow 100 L/s

$$\theta = \frac{H}{mc}$$

$$= \frac{9.88}{0.13} \text{ at } 74°C, \text{ air } 100 \text{ L/s, water } 0.15 \text{ L/s}$$

$= 76°C$ temperature difference in a 30°C ambient

$= 46°C$ air out as proven in climatic testing

Fig. 6 Vehicle speed versus body conductance

Fig. 5 Heater matrix

ed air and not fresh. This fact reduces the air on temperature from 52°C steady state to 24°C and hence reduces the required power to 8.14 kW.

Ambient 52°C in-car average 24°C, $\Delta T = 28$°C

Body conductance or heat gain
at 55 miles/h	2.24 kW
Driver + 1 passenger heat gain	0.24 kW
Miscellaneous heat gain at 55 miles/h	0.5 kW
Sun load at 900 W/m² (approx.)	1.5 kW
Total heat input	4.5 kW

Air density at 52°C = 1.1 kg/m³
Air density at 24°C = 1.3 kg/m³
Vehicle airflow at full cold = 140 L/s

Air outlet temperature to maintain 24°C average interior = 4°C; therefore $\Delta T = 48$°C:

Therefore evaporator performance to reduce air temperature by 48°C = 48 × 1.1 × 140 = 739 W
$$= 7.39 \text{ kW}$$

Total evaporator performance = 7.39 + 4.5
$$= 11.89 \text{ kW}$$

However, on full recirculated air $\Delta T = 20$°C. Therefore,

evaporator performance $= 20 \times 1.3 \times 140$
$$= 3.64 \text{ kW}$$
Total evaporator performance = 3.64 + 4.5
$$= 8.14 \text{ kW}$$

Within the evaporator is another type of temperature sensor; the type used here is an electronic semiconductor coupled with a small circuit to enable accurate linear measurement of temperature. This unit is placed inside the evaporator to measure the fin temperatures and its function is twofold. Firstly, it must control the air conditioning compressor by cycling its clutch as evaporative demand is met and, secondly, it must prevent the evaporator icing, which can be caused by the condensed water freezing within the fins of the evaporator. This must not occur as it prevents airflow and would eventually affect interior temperature and freon circuit performance.

Many peripherals are attached to the main case moulding. The air distribution to the feet is achieved using two plastic mouldings which slide into the front case sections (Fig. 8). These are easily detachable for access to the unit and for alternative designs if neces-

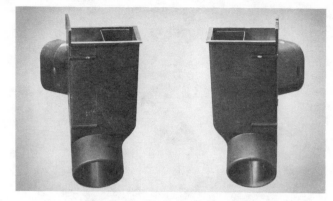

Fig. 8   Footwell distributor ducts

sary. They are also made from a talc-filled polypropylene.

Attached to the end of the rotary air valves are the drive motors. Two motors are used, one for each flap. They are small d.c. motors connected to each shaft via a worm gear and three spur gears, which are moulded in plastic to reduce both noise and weight and have a reduction ratio of 1500 : 1. This provides the torque strength to overcome seal friction at the extreme temperatures found inside the unit.

At the opposite end of the rotary air valves are the positional sensors. These are rotary potentiometers which form the return leg of a closed-loop system (Fig. 9). It is necessary for the drive motors to know at what position they must stop and this is provided by these potentiometers. The location was chosen to overcome any torsional twist occurring in the flap itself. The sensors are held on separate steel plates which are calibrated prior to unit fit, and this negates the need for awkward setting procedures at both production and service stages.

Suspended below the unit are four vacuum solenoids which control air vents and the water valve (Fig. 10). These are positioned on two removable plates for serviceability. The connecting harnesses carry vacuum restrictors which act as dynamic dampers on the moving vents. These prevent sudden changes in setting from the inherently fast operation of vacuum solenoids.

One other major component is attached to the case of the unit: the microprocessor itself (Fig. 11). The micro is a dedicated computer designed specifically for the air conditioning system. In production form it carries a masked 8 bit microcomputer within a support circuit of amplifiers, analogue to digital converters, resistors, capacitors, diodes and voltage regulators. The circuit is designed to fit in the smallest space and its shape has

Fig. 7   Evaporator

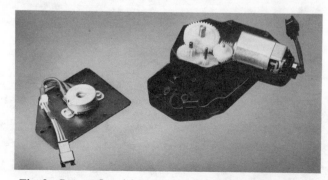

Fig. 9   Rotary flap drive motor and feedback potentiometer

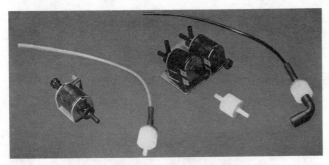

Fig. 10 Vacuum solenoids

been tailored to fit the contour of the main unit. The printed circuit board has used multi-layer techniques to assist with radiofrequency protection while the circuit design has been paramount in providing an intrinsically safe electrical unit for use in an automotive environment. The vehicle uses a number of microprocessors and it is necessary to protect each unit from interference and interfering with other units. The circuit, once built on to the board, is then conformally coated to protect against the environment. This also makes each unit tamperproof. It will in normal circumstances prevent unauthorized testing due to its all-enveloping nature. In the design of the system, this was considered and a 45 pin diagnostic access plug was built into the unit. This is compatible with the vehicle test equipment developed for the dealers and enables a full diagnosis test to be completed. Each processor is fully tested and functionally operated before it reaches the vehicle to ensure the high level of reliability required.

Surrounding and supporting the main unit are a number of items which combine to make a complete climate control system. The major parts are the air blowers (Fig. 12). There are two blower units mounted on either side of the main case. Each consists of a three-part plastic moulding in the same talc-filled polypropylene as the main case. The high-performance motor has been isolated from the casing to ensure low noise and carries a high level of balance at its production stage. The squirrel cage rotors have been designed for high air pressure with a low noise and these have been made in a sniamid material for low weight and good rigidity. Integral with the blower casing is a flap and actuation mechanism to alter the air intake mode from fresh interior air to recirculated air. This change is made upon demand of the microprocessor and is a vacuum function signalled from one of the previously mentioned vacuum solenoids. Within each blower is a heatsink assembly containing the elec-

tronic speed control devices which form the power side of the infinitely variable fan speed. The running signal is provided by the microprocessor, which is then actioned by the individual blower circuitry. To reduce voltage drop within the vehicle harness a relay is positioned within the blowers to allow direct power feed upon demand; this is effected during maximum performance requirements or defrost selections.

In the right-hand blower unit is another electronic semiconductor and circuit to measure temperature. This device is identical in performance to the unit mounted in the evaporator but in this instance it measures the ambient air temperature. The microprocessor uses this information to compensate for changes in exterior conditions which would affect the vehicle interior.

The control system can measure exterior ambients but it must also measure interior ambients. This is achieved using a third sensor of the same design, giving a linear voltage output for temperature change. The in-car sensor is mounted in the crash roll and has air forced across it by an aspiration system supplied from the right-hand blower outlet. The aspirator is a single plastic injection moulding.

To complete the sensing system (Fig. 13) a fourth sensor has been included. This unit is mounted in the top of the facia at the vehicle centre-line. Its function is to measure radiant sun load and enable the microprocessor to compensate for the direct heat load associated with high levels of sunlight. It uses a photo transistor and circuit housed in a button-sized plastic mount.

Control of the total system is via a switch pack mounted in the centre console (Fig. 14). This is the only part of the climate control system available to the user.

With a combination of rotary, slider and push button controls all variables and user options can be selected. The design of controls, their meanings and layout is a difficult and somewhat subjective field. Legislation too requires certain symbols to be included and various lighting conditions achieved. Consideration is therefore twofold: regulations must be met and the user must be catered for. The final design (Fig. 15) was based on an ergonomic survey and concept style for the options available from the unit. The need to retain the individuality of a Jaguar meant keeping a rotary control for

Fig. 11 Microprocessor

Fig. 12 Air blower

Fig. 13   Control system sensors

fan speeds and temperature select with the modern facilities added, via slider and push buttons.

To overcome transient changes in vehicle use a manual automatic override has been included which if operated gives the option of maintaining full heat output, full cold output or any set point in between, regardless of ambient conditions. Another area where optional change occurs is for air distribution. It is occasionally felt more air is required to the screen and this can now be achieved by selection of another push button. An economy device has been included which disconnects the air conditioning compressor on demand. This option would be used in cold climates as it turns the unit into a heater only. A second pair of buttons has been added to control the evaporator temperature. With these and the economy function the user may select a total of four variables for evaporator temperature. These are jointly called humidity control. The options have allowed control of the evaporator temperature at four different levels. The lowest control point is 0–0.25°C and would be used for maximum capacity cooling and high ambient conditions. This will remove the maximum amount of moisture from the air. The second control point is 3.9–4.15°C. The temperature control in-car is maintained but less moisture is removed from the air. This setting is ideal for medium ambient conditions. The third selection controls at 7.1–7.35°C and would be used in low ambient conditions. The fourth, and final, option is economy. The evaporator would reach ambient temperatures as described earlier.

Use of these functions will allow selected variation in the level of humidity in the car and may be altered for personal preference or ambient conditions. The set point of the evaporator will affect power consumption for the compressor: hence fuel economy may be gained without loss of air conditioning using these controls.

The last variable on the switch pack is operated by a slider. Its function is to alter the temperature difference between the face level and foot level without altering the in-car set point.

These are the option controls available to the user. The panel will retain any of these settings with an in-built memory function. There are, within the panel, two levels of illumination, one for control status and one for general lighting operated with the side lights.

Fig. 14   Control panel

Fig. 15   The final design on the centre console

The panel now meets legislation requirements and offers the user all variables available from the system.

7 DEVELOPMENT PROCESS

Development of the unit began on a rig. Here a series of prototype plastic components were assembled and run to prove the basic principles of a two-flap system. At the initial stages a simple analogue control was used.

The first processor chosen was a 3870 micro with a 2K EPROM facility. The software was developed around the basic unit design and specification taking into account the proposed feature level, sensors and controls. The software routine is shown in Fig. 16. Use of the processor enabled changes to be made quite simply as the software was written around a series of look-up tables. An emulator was produced to match the 3870 through which all our original development was run.

A series of environmental tests was conducted in some of the most severe conditions available. This involved the Arizona desert and the Canadian arctic. Temperatures varied from −38°C to a high of +49°C, so enabling complete testing to all forseeable extremes.

Many of the variables were changed during these tests and the processor was increased in capacity from the original 2K to 4K of memory. This became necessary as the software was developed, becoming more complex as problems were encountered and overcome.

During tests the sensors were modified around the vehicle and their effects modified until control criteria were met.

The calculation undertaken by the processor for a balance condition and hence no change is:

Balance

In-car temperature = temperature demand
$$\qquad\qquad - \text{solar load}$$
$$\qquad\qquad - \left(\frac{\text{ambient temperature} - 24}{10}\right)$$

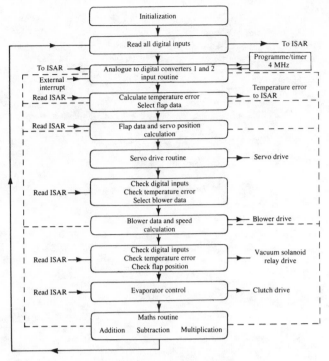

Fig. 16   The software routine

If an imbalance is found a temperature error is recorded and an output made to the servo drives and blower controls. For this condition the calculation becomes:

Imbalance

Temperature error = temperature demand

$$-\left[\text{in-car temperature} + \text{solar} + \left(\frac{\text{ambient temperature} - 24}{10}\right)\right]$$

Temperature demand and in-car temperature are the overriding factors throughout this calculation. The ambient sensor is a one-tenth divider for each degree beyond an average 24°C and the solar sensor has a maximum effect of 2°C below set point. The values for solar compensation were developed from the photoelectric response of the phototransistor during daily cycles

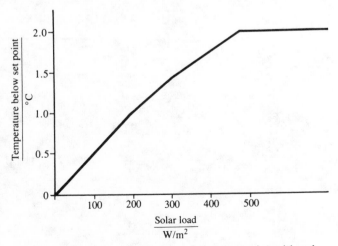

Fig. 17   Variation of temperature below set point with solar load

in the United States, Canada and the United Kingdom. The final specification is shown in Fig. 17.

Once an alteration had been made it was necessary to retest a batch of units to assess the effect on a production basis. As the unit became more refined in terms of tooled components so the effect of processor changes became more predictable.

The accuracy of the microprocessor and its ability to repeat conditions exactly brought with it some problems. The hardware and manufacturing tolerances of the system could not match that of the processor. This meant averaging results from groups of units to obtain the optimum processor settings to account for possible production variations. Monitoring of this condition is a requirement of the specification and will be an ideal control medium for production.

8 THE FINAL PRODUCT

To enable the unit to comply with original requirements meant a great deal of control throughout the production and development stages. To ensure correct build a series of jigs and fixtures are used and on-line diagnostic equipment, itself microprocessor controlled, developed.

The unit carried both a design and build failure mode effect analysis, which is continually being updated. Line trials were completed by both the manufacturer and Jaguar to assess all aspects of unit build and installation before full volume was reached.

Final in-house control on the system is achieved by rig test. It is a further requirement of this specification that units throughout the life of the vehicle undergo full performance checks.

It is also part of the the company system to monitor user/customer feedback for future modifications or features that become necessary.

The company's aim from concept to production has been to build a reliable and efficient unit to complement and enhance the total vehicle.

This has been achieved.

9 ACHIEVEMENTS

Performance—heat output increased by 6.2 per cent
 cold output increased by 19.4 per cent
 airflow increased by 33 per cent with stepless control

Reliability—FMEA processes completed
 rig endurance testing 20 000 cycles on units complete
 car endurance testing complete
 off tool component faults reduced

Weight—unit weight reduced by 7.2 per cent

Size—present package size maintained

Cost—reduction in cost by 30 per cent

ACKNOWLEDGEMENT

The author would like to thank the following for their assistance in the preparation of this paper and their work on the system: Delanair Limited, in particular Mr R. J. Thorburn; Gaydon Technology for their excellent facilities; and colleagues at Jaguar Cars Limited.

Development of an air mass flow sensing microprocessor-based fuelling and ignition system

A E Baxendale, BSc, MSc, CEng, MIMechE
Jaguar Cars Limited, Coventry

The philosophy for the choice of engine management systems for the Jaguar XJ40 is discussed, and certain features developed for the 3.6 litre engine are described in detail.

1 INTRODUCTION

At the concept stage the specification for the XJ40 engine management system was defined and certain features were considered to be essential.

Firstly, an electronic system, rather than mechanical, was required because of its superior flexibility of control and also its ease of adjustment in the development stage. Microprocessor-based digital systems represented the latest 'state-of-the-art' technology, and were therefore chosen. Such control flexibility provided by these systems was required in order to satisfy the various engine fuelling and ignition timing requirements, particularly the compromises that are involved in tuning for best economy, performance, drivability and, not least, exhaust emission control over the complete engine operating range.

Secondly, mass airflow sensing was defined as a requirement, in that to achieve the extreme accuracy of control it is necessary to compensate automatically for seasonal variations in ambient conditions of temperature and barometric pressure, as well as for altitude effects. Hot wire anemometer type airflow meters meet these requirements and are also fast in response to transient changes, which was another requirement laid down for the system in order to provide good drivability characteristics.

Finally, automatic idle speed control was required in order to allow lower idle speeds to be used than previously for the purpose of reducing the vehicle overall fuel consumption and improving engine refinement.

Two engine families were being developed concurrently for the XJ40, namely the 2.9 litre two-valve and the 3.6 litre four-valve versions of the same basic AJ6 power unit. Of the engine management systems available that met the above specification, the Bosch LH injection system was selected for the 2.9 litre engine and the Lucas 9CU combined ignition and fuelling system for the 3.6 litre.

The Bosch equipment was already fitted to other manufacturers' products at the start of the development programme, and therefore this was, in theory, a straightforward application exercise. In practice, however, there have been a number of changes made during the application, as Bosch advanced their system design and certain aspects of the programme were repeated. On the other hand, the Lucas system has been developed jointly with Jaguar, and therefore this paper

concentrates on the latter, and especially some of the features which are unique to this system. The system is shown diagrammatically in Fig. 1 and is also described in a paper by Cops (**1**).

2 SYSTEM DESCRIPTION

2.1 Hot wire air mass flow measurement

Hot wire anemometry has been adopted for automotive applications in recent times, and was chosen for the XJ40 for its ability to measure true mass flow. It is therefore able to compensate for the small variations in airflow characteristics from engine to engine which occur on series production units. It is also fast responding and presents minimum resistance to flow. Hence there was complete freedom to develop the induction system for maximum performance from the engine.

The air mass flow signal from the meter is converted into a measurement of mass flow per engine cycle, and this basic engine characteristic is then converted into a matrix of 16 speed by 8 load sites for the purpose of calibrating the fuelling and the ignition timing independently of each other. There is interpolation such that the calibration is progressive between sites.

The hot wire air meters used by Jaguar have also proved to be very durable, in that 5.5 million miles have been run on vehicles in various locations around the world, with virtually no failures.

2.2 Mapped digital ignition

Conventional distributor type ignition systems using mechanical bob weight advance mechanisms require considerable compromises to be made in the advance characteristics specified, particularly at full throttle. Generally engines require or can tolerate less ignition advance at the engine speed for maximum torque than they do at speeds either above or below this value. This condition therefore normally defines the maximum advance line for a centrifugal mechanism (see Fig. 2).

With a digital system, by careful selection of the speed sites for the mapped characteristics, account can be taken of the peaks and troughs in the advance requirement. Also a further advantage with a digital system is that secondary control functions such as coolant temperature, air inlet temperature and throttle position can be used to modify the basic map in order

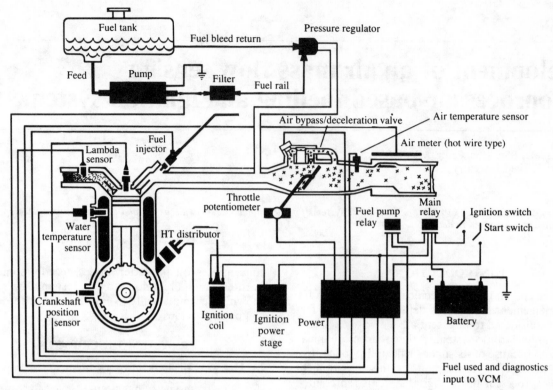

Fig. 1 Schematic of engine management system for the four-valve XJ40 engine [courtesy Lucas Electrical Company]

to optimize the engine for the purpose of exhaust emission control or to compensate for extremes of operating conditions.

One such secondary control feature on the XJ40 involves the use of ignition retard with high inlet air temperatures. During testing in the United Kingdom on the initially mapped ignition advance characteristic there was no sign of a problem with detonation. In fact early knock rating tests on the engine indicated a reasonable safety margin on commercially available European fuels. However in operating vehicles in the Arizona Desert at ambient temperatures of 45–50°C, detonation became evident. The detonation occurred at the usual critical speeds, as indicated in Fig. 2.

Bench tests to define the sensitivity of the detonation borderline to air inlet temperature gave a retard characteristic which could readily be matched by the control unit. However in the field this amount of retard applied

over the whole map detracted unacceptably from the vehicle performance. Thus a characteristic which retards only in the critical areas has been specified (see Fig. 3). Three degrees of retard is applied per 10 degrees increase in air inlet temperature above the reference temperature of 30°C. This is only applied from 3000 r/min upwards and at the higher engine loads.

2.3 Mapped digital fuelling

The fuelling calibration for the engine when operating fully warm is defined in a similar manner to that for the ignition, namely by a 16×8 airflow matrix. Starting and warm-up characteristics consist of factors applied to the fully warm fuelling, as does the acceleration enrichment which is initiated by rotation of the throttle potentiometer attached to the throttle butterfly spindle.

Other transient functions are treated as below.

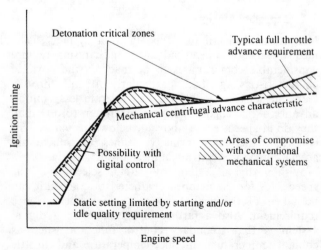

Fig. 2 Ignition versus speed map

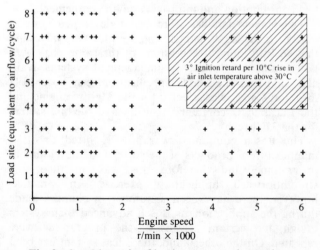

Fig. 3 8×16 matrix of load versus speed map sites

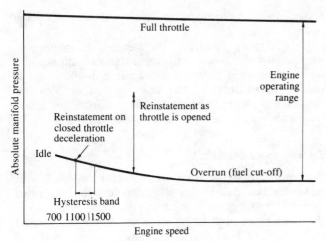

Fig. 4   Fuel cut-off and reinstatement

2.4 Fuel cut-off reinstatement

Fuel cut-off is used for the improvement in fuel economy that it provides, and also for the control of exhaust emissions. In operation the fuel is cut off, or injection ceases, when the engine speed is above 1100 r/min and the throttle is closed, provided that the deceleration started from above 1500 r/min. This higher speed or hysteresis is set in order to prevent cycling in and out of fuel cut-off when decelerating down to rest on a closed throttle. This means that the engine speed has to rise to 1500 r/min after fuel reinstatement before cut-off can be obtained again. Figure 4 demonstrates this function, showing how it is controlled both by engine speed and by throttle position.

A problem with fuel cut-off, which digital fuelling and ignition has helped to overcome, is the driveline oscillation that can occur in response to the step change in engine power output between fuel off and fuel on, and vice versa (see Fig. 5). To soften the transition the ignition timing is temporarily retarded at the instant of fuel reinstatement and the fuelling is trimmed weak momentarily at that instant, thus reducing engine power output.

2.5 Closed-loop fuelling control

Closed-loop fuelling control that is used with three-way catalyst applications applies to the United States, Japan, Australia, Switzerland, Austria, Sweden and, as an option, the German markets. It operates in a digital manner, and it is possible to change the time constants of the system to suit the various requirements involving exhaust emission control and engine stability (see Fig. 6). The time constants, and hence amplitude of fuelling oscillation, are determined by the relative sizes of the steps RI, RS, LI and LS, and on the XJ40 these are different between idle and off idle.

To explain the operation of the feedback system in more detail, the fuelling is mapped in the normal way, such that the fuel delivery is appropriate for the load and speed at that particular instant. The part-load fuelling is calibrated to give a stoichiometric air–fuel ratio, rather than minimum specific fuel consumption or optimum raw emissions, which would be the case on an open-loop system. However the air–fuel ratio cannot be maintained accurately enough at stoichiometric for the

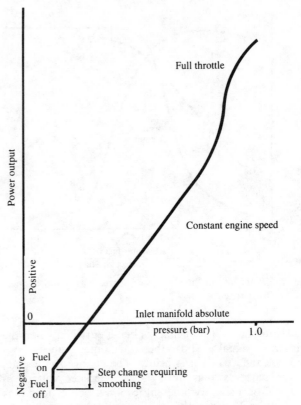

Fig. 5   Fuel cut-off effect on engine power output

catalyst to function continuously at all conditions. A small deviation in the air–fuel ratio causes the catalyst to cease oxidizing or reducing, as the case may be, depending upon the direction of deviation (see Fig. 7).

To achieve the necessary accuracy the oxygen sensor measures the exhaust oxygen content and gives an output as shown also in Fig. 6, varying from 200 mV at weaker than stoichiometric to 800 mV at richer than stoichiometric. This signal orders the electronic control unit (ECU) to provide compensating enrichment when the fuelling is weaker than stoichiometric, and enleanment when it is richer.

The output which indicates the fuelling condition is also shown in Fig. 6, and this is referred to as the feed-

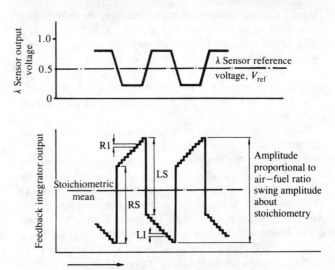

Fig. 6 V_{ref}, RI, RS, LI and LS are all variable to provide rich or lean bias from stoichiometry to suit catalyst performance characteristic

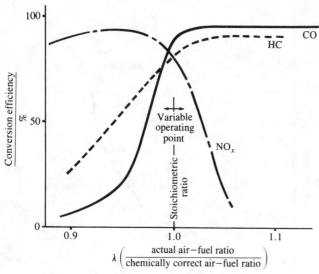

Fig. 7 Effect of air–fuel ratio on three-way catalyst performance

back integrator. The fuelling is being enriched when the integrator signal is above the stoichiometric mean level and enleaned when it is below. The changeover occurs as the sensor swings through the reference voltage of 500 mV, or a slightly different level if a rich or lean bias is required, for example the integrator changes from putting fuel on to taking it off, as step LS occurs. Step LI then occurs, once every ignition spark, until the oxygen sensor detects that the fuelling error is in the opposite direction, thus causing step RS to occur. The value of these large and small steps are chosen so as to control the amplitude of fuelling swing, particularly at idle, and also to suit the catalyst performance characteristics with regard to perturbation requirement and also whether it is required to perform more of an oxidizing or reducing role. This adjustment provides a second method for creating rich or lean bias from stoichiometric, as may be required depending upon whether the engine is a higher NO_x emitter than HC, or vice versa.

2.6 Fuelling adaptation

The ECU also has an adaptive feature, in that it can learn that a setting has changed, or is not ideal, and make an adjustment to the memory to compensate. One such feature concerns the setting of the throttle potentiometer, which controls idle fuelling, fuel cut-off and full load fuelling. This normally needs to be set precisely, particularly from the point of view of fuel cut-off control.

With the adaptive system the minimum output from the potentiometer is memorized. This corresponds to the closed throttle position needed for the control of the above functions, and is therefore used as the reference for this purpose. To ensure that the adaptive feature only responds to throttle potentiometer variation at closed throttle, it can only function with the engine speed below 1000 r/min and the vehicle speed below 3 miles/h. Furthermore, the adaptation only operates over a limited potentiometer output range, thus preventing a steady cruise condition being detected as closed throttle. However, with this function the potentiometer no longer needs to be very accurately positioned with

respect to the throttle butterfly, as was previously the case.

This adaptive feature of the system has many possibilities for the future with regard to fuel supply and ignition timing. However, considerable development is needed to ensure that the adaptive system does not cause adjustments to be made when they are not necessary, or when they are positively undesirable.

2.7 Idle speed control

With normal engine applications the idle speed has to be set high enough for the engine to sustain the various electrical and hydraulic loads applied to it at idle all at the same time, both under steady state conditions and also transiently when coming down to rest, without stalling. Thus under lighter loaded conditions the idle speed is higher than it needs to be, and hence more fuel is being consumed than is necessary.

The Lucas microprocessor engine management system incorporates a closed-loop idle speed control utilizing a stepper motor operated valve situated in a throttle bypass port. The control system only operates closed-loop under limited conditions, namely when (a) the throttle is closed, (b) the fuel system is not in fuel cut-off and (c) the road speed is below 5 miles/h. However, under open-loop operation, which applies when any of the above prerequisites are not satisfied, the stepper motor continually adjusts to an idle run line, dependent upon whether the transmission is in drive or neutral and whether the air conditioning is clutched in or not. It is further adjusted according to coolant temperature (see Fig. 8). This calibration in its various forms is aimed at providing the nominal idle speed under all conditions, and hence leaving the feedback system with the minimum of correction to make when the feedback loop is eventually closed.

The closed-loop operation of the control system is adaptive, in that any correction found necessary to the run line to obtain the control idle speed is memorized and used as the datum for any further adjustment of the run line with coolant temperature or engine load. Hence even if the base idle speed goes slightly out of adjustment, the feedback system will bring it back into line. The only proviso is that the feedback system has a

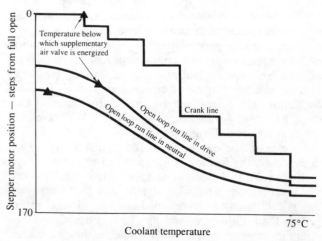

Fig. 8 Idle speed control stepper motor operating characteristics during open-loop mode

limited range of adjustment, and can therefore only make a relatively small correction.

Due to limitations on the flow capacity of the idle speed control valve, it was found necessary to use a supplementary air valve to satisfy the air requirements of the engine at relatively low sub-zero temperatures. This valve is a simple solenoid-operated on/off valve and is energized as shown in Fig. 8.

A further open-loop characteristic is provided which gives twelve positions for the stepper motor during cranking, the position being dependent upon coolant temperature. Thus the airflow into the engine under starting conditions can also be optimized for minimum start time.

The actual control idle speed on a closed loop is higher during engine warm-up, to give a stronger idle, thus compensating for more severe transient loads under these conditions (see Fig. 9). The closed-loop operation of the system has to be carefully matched to prevent surging of the idle speed if the response is too quick, or overshooting if the response is too slow. To this end it has been found necessary to have a dead band around the chosen idle speed, in which no correction is made. Outside this band is a narrow slow response area which prevents rapid surging of the engine, and then further outside this the response is quick. The latter allows for rapid correction of large errors in idle speed, both high and low (see Fig. 10).

2.8 Air injection system control

Air injection is used on the specifications fitted with exhaust catalysts in order to achieve some oxidation of the carbon monoxide and unburnt hydrocarbons in the exhaust manifold, and, more importantly, to increase the warm-up rate of the catalyst at the start of the exhaust emission test, since the catalyst has to reach around 350°C before it begins to control the exhaust emissions.

As the air pump is only needed very briefly from cold it is fitted with a magnetic clutch, which enables it to be disengaged when not required. The switching of the air pump clutch is controlled by the engine management ECU, which provides air injection when the coolant temperature is between 15 and 38°C and the engine speed is below 2500 r/min.

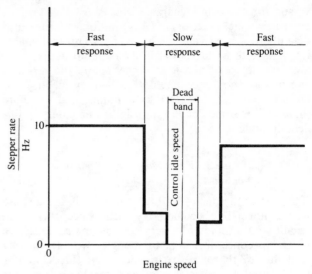

Fig. 10 Idle speed control stepper motor response characteristics

2.9 Trip computer interface

The ECU has an interface with the trip computer, in that it provides pulses from which the vehicle fuel consumption is calculated. These pulses are dependent upon the actual injector pulse duration at the time and their frequency. The output of the trip computer is in the form of 50 000 pulses/Imp gallon.

2.10 Self-diagnostic and limp-home feature

The system has the ability to detect whether all the input signals to the ECU are sensible, and, if they are not, to indicate a warning on the instrument pack that there is a 'fault'. When this occurs 'fuelling failure' is indicated while the vehicle is in motion, and a particular fault code is displayed the next time that the driver goes to start the engine, but prior to cranking and providing that the ignition has previously been off for at least 10 seconds. In these circumstances the fuel system can assume an average value for that erroneous input signal and thus allow the driver to get home before arranging to have the fault corrected.

The following problems, listed against the instrument pack fault code, can be detected, and the relevant action taken by the ECU is described.

2.10.1 Fault code 1. Spurious crank signal

The ECU receives a signal from the starter motor crank relay, which is used to initiate fuelling enrichment during starting. This signal is normally inhibited by the ECU above 400 r/min. However, if a signal is detected when the engine is (a) rotating at greater than 2000 r/min or (b) cranking but not generating a crankshaft trigger signal, it is assumed that a fault exists, and the signal is ignored. Fault code 1 will be generated and will be displayed on the instrument pack when the ignition is next switched on.

2.10.2 Fault code 2. Air meter signal open circuit or earthed

If the air meter signal is open circuit or earthed, the ECU detects this and a precalibrated engine speed

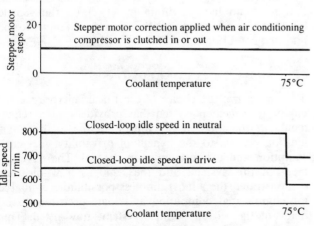

Fig. 9 Idle speed control during warm-up

versus throttle angle characteristic is used instead to determine fuel delivery. The ignition timing also defaults to a fixed value of 20° BTDC. This will enable the vehicle to be driven safely over the normally available engine speed and load range, before the repair is effected. It should be noted that neither fuelling nor ignition timing will be set to optimum and therefore there will be some deterioration in fuel economy in this default mode.

2.10.3 Fault code 3. Water temperature sensor open or short circuit

If the water thermistor lead were to fall off, the fuelling would normally become very rich, since this open circuit would represent a very cold engine as far as the ECU was concerned. In fact the engine would probably stall due to the excessive richness. On the XJ40 this fault would be detected and a water temperature of 30°C would be assumed for all running conditions and −30°C for cranking. This would enable the vehicle to be driven from 0°C or lower, to fully warm, with the possibility of a start down to −30°C, with little effect on drivability from a relatively low part-warm condition. However, the fully warm fuelling would be rather richer than necessary or desired.

The starting enrichment was chosen as −30°C to enable starts to be obtained at very low temperatures in this fault condition. To prevent overfuelling at the higher temperatures a facility was incorporated to inhibit cranking fuel when the throttle is held fully open. Thus, as a bonus, there is a means to overcome inadvertent flooding of the engine, which might otherwise preclude a start being obtained.

2.10.4 Fault code 4. Fuelling feedback system inoperative

It will become a legal requirement in California in 1988 for vehicles using feedback systems on the fuelling control to indicate if/when the feedback fails to function. This legislation was considered necessary by California Air Resources Board because the driver probably would be unaware of the fault and the exhaust emission levels for one or more of the pollutants could become an order of magnitude higher than the legal standard.

The system on the XJ40 meets this requirement, a fault being indicated when the feedback system is detected not to be oscillating about the stoichiometric fuelling. This has needed careful tuning to select the sensitivity of the fault warning system, because there are occasions when the feedback may fail to function without a fault. This is particularly so when considering the fuel tank evaporative loss control system fitted for many markets and gradually becoming a requirement throughout the world. In these cases the vapour, which is discharged from the fuel tank as the bulk fuel temperature rises due to increased ambient temperature or to heat picked up in the recirculating fuel system, has to be consumed by the engine.

This additional fuel is unmetered as far as the engine is concerned, and although the feedback system attempts to compensate for this enriching of the mixture, a time can come when it fails to maintain control. Thus a time function has to be built into the

fault detection system, so that the feedback has to cease to switch for a certain period before the fault is indicated. The time constant chosen before feedback failure is indicated is 60 000 engine revolutions for rich excursions from stoichiometric and 1000 revolutions for weak excursions, that is it is also engine speed dependent. This fuel tank vent consideration is only significant in extremely hot climates or where very volatile fuels are used.

2.10.5 Fault code 5. Low throttle pot/high air meter voltages

This fault system looks for an incompatibility of two sensor outputs, namely the throttle potentiometer and the air meter. It is reasoned that it is impossible to obtain a high air meter output with the throttle closed. If this occurs the ECU disregards the throttle potentiometer signal, and hence idle speed control, idle trim, fuel cut-off and acceleration enrichment are all disabled.

2.10.6 Fault code 6. High throttle pot/low air meter voltages

Similar logic is used for this fault warning, and again the throttle potentiometer signal is ignored, with the same consequences.

With this feature it was found necessary to retune the fault detection to accommodate high-altitude operation and the effect that the reduced air density has on the air meter signal.

2.10.7 Fault code 7. Idle trim pot short circuit or 5 volts

This would normally result in an idle trim setting error causing the fuelling to go fully rich or lean. On the XJ40 the fault would be indicated on the instrument pack, but the idle fuelling would revert to the nominal setting and should therefore be more appropriate for the average engine.

2.10.8 Fault code 8. Air temperature sensor open or short circuit

The air temperature sensor is used to provide local ignition retard at high ambient temperature where detonation may become a problem. If the sensor becomes open or short circuit, the ignition timing defaults to that for the reference temperature of 30°C. This was chosen so that it would have a minimum effect on the vehicle full-throttle performance, rather than to default into the retarded condition.

3 CONCLUSIONS

To summarize, the choice of the Lucas microprocessor engine management system has provided many refinements in the method of controlling the fuelling and ignition timing, to the benefit of drivability, fuel consumption and exhaust emission control. The development of this system, and the XJ40 as a whole, has demonstrated the almost limitless possibilities available for complicated computing and logic decisions to be made in the various vehicle systems now fitted. This power has also enabled most circuits to be provided with a fail safe feature, together with a comprehensive self-diagnostic facility, which should speed up fault location and repair.

ACKNOWLEDGEMENTS

The author wishes to thank his colleagues, Mr G. W. Jones and Mr R. Purvis, for support in the preparation of this paper and Mr S. Otto of Lucas for his help in ensuring the technical accuracy of the description of the various ECU circuit functions.

REFERENCE

1 **Cops, M. H.** Developments in electronic control of engine management. Presented at the IMechE Conference on Automotive Electronics, 1985 (to be published).

Development of a service support system for microprocessor-controlled vehicle electrical systems

M J Andrews, BEng, AMIEE and **A D Clarke**
Jaguar Cars Limited, Coventry

This paper describes the development of a diagnostic system for the service support of the microprocessor-controlled electrical systems for the Jaguar XJ40. It includes details of the system concept, specification, hardware, software structure and operator interfaces.

1 BACKGROUND

In recent years, automotive electrical systems have become increasingly sophisticated and complex in their application of electrical/electronic systems with a view to satisfy, progressively, more demanding reliability, emissions, performance, economy, and customer feature requirements. This is particularly apparent in the case of the XJ40 model.

Following in the train of this growth of complexity has been an international car dealer body trying to keep pace with fast-moving product technology. This has been compounded by vehicle design engineers failing to take account of systems testability and the absence of a comprehensive strategic approach to vehicle diagnosis and test. Thus there is the potential for unnecessarily long customer off-the-road times and significant levels of component warranty claims which subsequent investigation may reveal to be serviceable items.

In addition it was reasonable to conjecture that the more reliable the vehicle system, the greater the need for a comprehensive diagnostic approach, because fewer vehicle faults would mean a corresponding reduction in familiarity with the system. Consequently technicians could become progressively less practised in diagnostic techniques.

Earlier approaches to systems test equipment have been based on hard wired, analogue devices such as, in Jaguar's case, Epitest, Pectron (air conditioning tester), cruise control testers and ignition system testers. These devices, though serving a useful purpose, are essentially flawed in a number of respects, but particularly in one area of overriding importance—flexibility. The hard wired approach dictates that if a design change is introduced on models in current production which affects the interface with or testability of the system concerned, the test equipment *must be modified*. The logistics, expense and equipment downtime associated with such a modification, taking into account the international spread of the equipment, may lead to inconvenience and high cost to the dealer.

Thus during the development phase of the XJ40 it was vital to create a test strategy which would place dealers in an excellent position to provide customers with the levels of service necessary to support not only the XJ40 model but future new products, while avoiding subsequent unnecessary recapitalization of dealer workshops. This in turn would lead to increased customer satisfaction, repeat sales and a marked reduction in poor diagnosis and warranty costs.

Such a strategy was evolved and has culminated in the creation of the Jaguar Diagnostic System (JDS). The evolution of this system is discussed in subsequent paragraphs.

2 THE XJ40 ELECTRICAL SYSTEM

The electrical system used on the XJ40 is in many ways radically different from that seen on vehicles to date. This is particularly evident in the use of high technology components and systems which are described elsewhere in these papers.

Limited facilities for vehicle self-diagnosis have been incorporated, but as each major vehicle system is substantially independent of its associates, this approach could not be applied to any significant extent. The major vehicle microprocessor-based systems are:

Central timer/logic control
Engine management
Instrumentation
Air conditioning
Cruise control
Anti-lock braking

In addition, a number of discrete logic modules perform auxiliary functions such as lighting and audible warnings. Each microprocessor system contains a 'watchdog' function to monitor the microchip itself and provide a system restart if malfunction is detected. This provides a substantial level of system self-check, the only higher levels existing within the four-valve engine management unit, which has a limited system self-check function and fault retention capability.

Each major system is largely self-contained with little interface between systems. Differences exist in the input and output circuit configurations and current/voltage levels between such systems.

These factors lead to great difficulty in diagnosis unless a custom designed test system is available. The differences between vehicle systems leads to the requirement that custom test equipment be sufficiently flexible to handle all input/output configurations.

Diagnosis with 'conventional' equipment typified by the 'Avometer' is both difficult and in some cases impossible. Logic level differences are such that in certain systems 5 V is a circuit 'on' condition when in others it is 'off'. If diodes are used in a circuit/harness, open or short circuit can be obtained dependent upon which way the meter is connected.

The foregoing points to the necessity for XJ40 service facilities to be provided with an automatic test system for the correct diagnosis of faults.

3 THE APPROACH/STRATEGY

The two major factors required to diagnose a fault in an electrical system are:

(a) visibility, the ability to take measurements on or observe the status of the system,
(b) control, the ability to change the status of the system.

The level of visibility and control must be sufficient to diagnose which component of the system is at fault.

Such a statement raises four main issues:

1. In deriving a diagnosis technique, all likely modes of failure of the XJ40 electrical system were to be included. In the event of a functional error, the unit should correctly identify the electronic module, harness, switchgear element or electromechanical LRU (lowest replaceable unit) at fault. When diagnosing harness faults the system should recognize illegal harness open circuits and short circuits either to ground or battery supply voltage.

   To meet these requirements, the system must be able to individually discriminate all signal types within the vehicle. The nature of the XJ40 earth line switching design philosophy is such that special emphasis should be given to the checking of earth points.
2. It was necessary to determine the depth to which diagnosis should be implemented. As dealerships do not have the equipment or skill required to service printed circuit boards it was determined that diagnosis should not proceed beyond indicting the LRU level as any further detail would be superfluous. For example, the JDS should not diagnose which component inside an electronic module is faulty as rectification is generally by replacement of the complete module.
3. How should the JDS approach the vehicle's electromechanical components? Many components have an electrical constituent which is either dependent on a mechanically derived input, such as a fuel level sensor, or provides a mechanical output, for example a window lift system. To provide complete diagnosis of these components the JDS would require many complex and expensive electromechanical sensors. Consequently, the JDS only checks the electrical function of the component and if no fault is found the operator must check the mechanical function using conventional and well-understood techniques.
4. To what level of accuracy should the JDS be able to diagnose faults? While the theoretical ideal is, of course, 100 per cent, an initial objective was set at better than 95 per cent accuracy.

Additionally, it was necessary to consider the approach to sensor calibration. It was obviously desir-

able to avoid comparative techniques involving off-car reference standards. Thus it was determined adequate merely to check that the electrical output of a sensor is within its 'legal' range. The nature of the majority of the vehicle's sensors confirmed that this strategy was rational.

4 JDS HARDWARE CAPABILITY

Having discussed the technical objectives and parameters for the JDS, it was then necessary to determine what signals needed to be monitored or simulated and hence how the JDS hardware capability needed to be defined.

The XJ40 electrical system uses principles totally new to the automotive industry. These include:

1. Low-current earth line switching. The majority of the driver-operated controls switch to earth instead of to battery positive and only carry a small signal current, usually to a processor which controls the load.
2. Remote load current switching. Load currents are switched by a relay located close to the load. The relay is controlled by a low-current output from a processor or switch.
3. Poled processor inputs. The XJ40 uses a method of scanning switches to monitor their status, that is open or closed, frequently employed on computer keyboards.

This final point highlighted a further question. What signal types were present in the XJ40 electrical system?

Two state signals, for example switch and relay inputs and outputs
Frequencies, for example wheel speed and engine speed sensors
Pulse trains—fuel consumption, fuelling failures
Analogue signals—gauge inputs, air mass flow, servo position transducers

The dedicated hardware design of the JDS must be able to monitor and simulate where necessary these signal types and allow for future design changes to the XJ40 electrical system and new vehicles, perhaps using a different electrical approach. This hardware must in turn be controlled by a test engine also capable of:

(a) providing a display to the operator,
(b) implementing the software test programme,
(c) being updated in line with vehicle design changes,
(d) providing a hard-copy output of the fault description,
(e) being supported and serviced worldwide.

Having taken account of the nature of the vehicle's electrical system and the repairer's requirements for flexibility and ease of update it was apparent that the test solution would have to be created around a microprocessor-based test engine.

Further consideration led inevitably to the conclusion that the software should reside on an easily updatable media. However, a degree of robustness would be required, bearing in mind the nature of the environment in which it would be used. Thus a decision in principle was taken to utilize plastic-cased 3.5 inch floppy discs.

Data transfer from a host computer to the JDS was considered but, due to the uncertain nature of international data communications in some markets in which the JDS would operate, was at that stage discounted. The system nonetheless should have sufficient expansion capability to include this feature at a later date if required.

5 THE BASE PROCESSOR

The company had a choice of either finding an existing base processor that matched its requirements or having one custom designed. The latter, though providing an ideal solution, would have involved not only hardware design and development but a concurrent software language development, as well as the application of that hardware/software to the vehicle. Both time and cost constraints eliminated this approach.

A number of alternative established microprocessor-based packages were considered prior to arriving at the chosen solution, which is based upon an existing product from GenRad Inc., a leading company in the automatic test equipment market.

The base processor chosen, GenRad's Universal Field Tester, was selected for a number of key reasons:

1. It is designed to be capable of interfacing to an exceptionally wide range of test subjects, having a flexible input/output design.
2. It was originally developed as a portable test system and was found to be rugged in construction and able to tolerate an unusually wide range of environmental conditions.
3. As a runtime test system it is designed for dynamic testing and control of digital logic-based equipment.
4. Its software architecture is purpose designed to allow optimum implementation of automated test programmes in a user friendly way.
5. The system design offers suitable opportunities for future enhancement to cater for alternative vehicle electronics technologies, communications etc.
6. The supplying company's ability to offer worldwide field support through its network of service locations.
7. Ease of software updatability for the end user.
8. Flexible screen display.

Development of the custom input/output (I/O) hardware and the diagnostic software was undertaken by Cirrus Designs, based in Manchester, a subsidiary of GenRad Inc. who specialize in systems applications of GenRad's standard products, and a development contract was signed to provide this service.

Earlier the signal types found on the vehicle were discussed. Having found a suitable base processor, access to the vehicle's system had to be more closely analysed.

6 ACCESS TO THE VEHICLE ELECTRICAL SYSTEM

To gain the necessary test visibility of the XJ40 electrical system the points at which the JDS could gain access to the system had to be defined. The obvious point of access to gain maximum functional information on the system is at the control module or electronic control unit (ECU), that is the point of maximum test visibility. Only the air conditioning ECU has a diagnostic plug for monitoring all its inputs and outputs. The two engine management and the anti-lock braking ECUs have conventional 25- or 35-way connectors used on many existing vehicle systems.

The instrument pack and central timer/logic ECUs both use the positive-mate high density (PMHD) unsealed connectors designed specifically for the XJ40 project. To gain access to the I/O signals, the JDS must T-in to these connectors and therefore must have the appropriate connectors to mate with those on the vehicle. Although the JDS need only access one of the sub-systems at a time, due to their functional independence, it must be able to monitor all the I/O of the sub-system central processor. This defined a parallel I/O capability of 72 lines. The T-in was effected by using a 'pod' which contained all the appropriate connectors to allow the JDS to be connected into the system under test (see Fig. 1).

Having determined from the T-in point that there was a fault in one of the I/O lines being monitored, the JDS then needed a method of tracing the fault along the vehicle harness and associated connectors to locate the cause. This necessitated the use of two probes.

The first is a measurement probe. This has the ability to probe connectors in the harness to take voltage or resistance measurements as required by the software and to drive signals, both analogue and frequencies, into the harness, for example to provide a speed signal when testing the cruise control system. Its shape was the result of lengthy investigation into the ergonomic considerations of accessing vehicle connectors (see Fig. 2). Development of this probe is described in greater detail later in this paper.

The second is a current probe. This is a Hall-effect non-intrusive current measuring device. Unlike a multimeter which has to be connected in series with the current to be measured, the current probe only has to be clipped round the wire. It then senses the magnetic field which is proportional to the current flow (see Fig. 3).

7 THE FIRST DEVELOPMENT PHASE

The JDS then entered a phase of development to T-in into the vehicle harness. During this phase several problems became obvious:

1. A high lifetime terminal would have to be developed for the PMHD connector adapters used on the JDS itself. They must withstand at least 10 000 make and breaks, maintaining a low contact resistance and not damaging the vehicle's connector terminals. A gold-plated spring-loaded terminal was identified as being suitable.
2. There are six types of PMHD—36-, 24-, 15-, 6-, 4- and 2-way derivatives—each having male and female halves and many having inhibit pins to prevent incorrect insertion of connectors of a similar type located in close proximity. The JDS would require adaptors for all these, needing approximately 100 male and female high-life terminals. The PMHD housings used on the vehicle would also have to be modified both in material and design for use as adaptors. All the above considerations also apply to the positive-mate (PM) high-current sealed connector used on the XJ40.

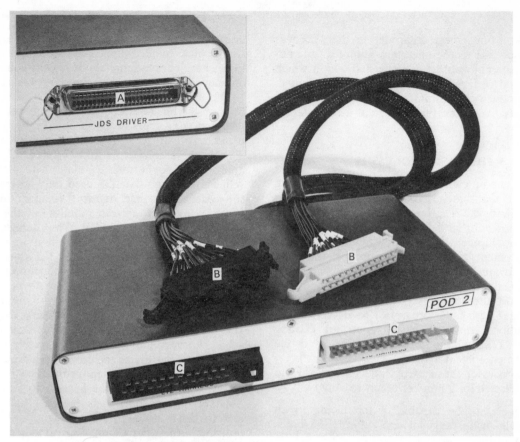

Fig. 1 3.6 litre engine management system pod. The system has four other pods: utilities; 2.9 litre engine management system; air conditioning/heater system; anti-lock braking system

    Key   A   Connection to JDS
                B   Connections to ECU
                C   Connections to vehicle harness

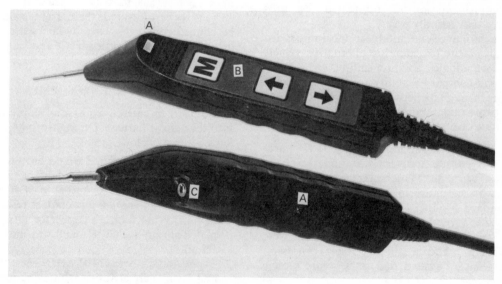

Fig. 2   Measurement probe

    Electrical specification
    $0 \rightarrow 20$ V range (± 20 mV basic accuracy)
    $0 \rightarrow 6.5$ kΩ resistance range with respect to ground or battery

    Key   A   'Contact confirmed' LEDS
                B   Membrane keypad
                     M   (measure)
                     ↑   (next)
                     ↓   (previous)
                C   Probe tip illumination

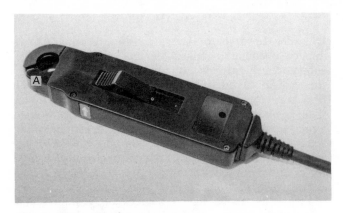

Fig. 3 Current probe

Electrical specification
100 mA → 10 A range (± 50 mA basic accuracy)

Auto-zero, to eliminate the effects of stray magnetic fields

Auto-degaussing, to prevent the permanent magnetization of the probe from starter motor currents

Key
A Moving jaw

3. In the event of a vehicle system requiring abnormally frequent diagnostic access, early test results suggested that vehicle connector make-and-break life could be exceeded. This factor was considered significant in a subsequent review of the T-in technique.
4. The T-in approach is an invasive access to the system, that is the electrical system, namely the connectors, needs to be disturbed. This may remove the possible cause of the fault—the connector itself—a high-probability fault area in any electrical system, whether on a vehicle or not.

8 A REVIEW OF THE APPROACH

After six months of development work on this approach it was necessary to reconsider the technique to avoid these problems. A feasibility study was carried out to determine whether it was still possible to diagnose faults on the vehicle without the test visibility provided by a T-in approach.

The main result of this study was that the T-in or 'pod' approach must be retained on both engine management ECUs and the anti-lock braking and air conditioning ECUs because:

(a) of their complex input/output relationship, that is one output is controlled by many inputs, the output in turn being fed back as an input, and
(b) they are timing critical systems, an output timing is related to other input(s) or output(s) event(s).

In these four instances the need to keep a 'pod' approach outweighed the disadvantages of invasive access, and connector durability on all but the air conditioning ECU was of less concern. A high lifetime connector was therefore developed for the air conditioning 'pod'.

The parallel I/O requirement of the JDS was reduced as a result of this modified approach to 42 lines

The T-in approach could be replaced by a functional approach on the remaining systems using PM4 and PMHD connections to their ECUs. With a functional approach the measurement and current probes are the main source of electrical measurements on the vehicle.

9 THE SECOND DEVELOPMENT PHASE

During the second phase of the project, based on the revised approach, the hardware shown in Figs 1 to 5 was developed. The system design evolved in recognition of the environmental and climatic conditions known to exist in dealer workshops around the world. During the JDS development and validation, it underwent stringent environmental and durability tests involving exposure to humidity, dust vibration, mechanical shock and automotive fluids, as well as many hundreds of hours of use in vehicle workshops.

Therefore the two major factors required for a successful diagnosis—'visibility' and 'control'—were achieved.

For JDS the sources of 'visibility' are:

The operator
Measurement probe
Current probe
Pods
Serial data from ECUs

and of 'control' are:

The operator
Measurement probe
Pods
Serial data to ECUs

Fig. 4 Keypad (keys F1 and F2 are for future requirements)

Key
A Membrane keypad

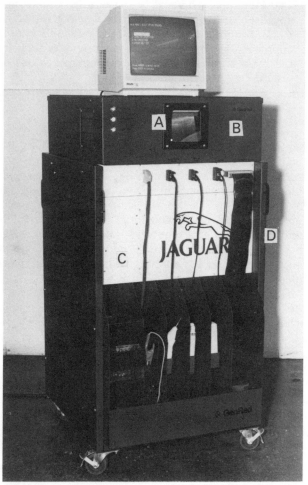

Fig. 5 The complete JDS

> *Key* A Base processor with:
>   (a) Z80A microprocessor (4 MHz clock)
>   (b) 512K DRAM
>   (c) 5 in CRT display
>   (d) double-sided double density disc drive 800K
>   formatted storage
>   (e) video output for an additional monitor
>   (f) RS232 serial communication port
>   (g) battery-backed real-time clock
>   (h) four-card expansion port
>   B Device specific adapter (DSA), using two cards of
>   the 2610 four-card expansion port. This is the
>   main interface from the processor to the vehicle
>   system, custom designed with the following fea-
>   tures:
>   (a) 42 input/output lines
>   (b) high current drive on selected lines
>   (c) 6801 processor
>   (d) pulse catcher
>   (e) edge detection
>   (f) peak hold
>   (g) frequency measurement and drive
>   (h) probe control and drive circuitry
>   (i) 10 bit analogue/digital converter
>   (j) 8 bit digital/analogue converters (three off)
>   C Printer, 40 column to provide hard-copy output
>   of the diagnosis
>   D Mobile cabinet including:
>   (a) air filters
>   (b) cooling fans
>   (c) thermal cut-out
>   (d) earth leakage circuit breaker
>   (e) storage for pods, probes, adapters, discs etc.

10 SOFTWARE

In order to develop the diagnostic software, Cirrus applied a common strategy in analysing each vehicle sub-system. Firstly, they obtained all necessary data on the vehicle circuit, not only the relevant component drawings but suppliers' circuit diagrams, end-of-line test data, including test limits and functional descriptions. From this information total sub-system arrangements were constructed. Each sub-system was broken down into function circuits consisting of its circuit elements, for example, a processor output, the load, the interconnecting wire (part of a harness) and connectors.

From the above list of sources of 'visibility' and 'control' the main area of possible error is the operator whom the JDS has no direct control over. To reduce this possibility the following constraints were placed on the software:

1. Minimum operator intervention:
   (a) The operator is not required to make technical decisions as a result of the JDS taking measurements using the probes or pods. The JDS makes the decisions in the diagnostic routine itself by comparing the measurements taken with its own stored reference data. This also eliminates the need for the operator to have detailed knowledge of the vehicle's electrical system.
   (b) The operator is required to operate the vehicle switchgear, perform visual checks and connect the JDS hardware to the vehicle as required. This is controlled by the JDS via its visual output in the form of questions and messages.
2. Minimum probing. The diagnostic routines are designed to minimize the amount of probing required to arrive at a diagnosis. During validation it has become clear that trim removal, the location and unclipping of connectors to allow probing, is the main factor in determining the time taken for a diagnosis, so minimum probing also means minimum labour costs.
3. Minimum connector opening. During a diagnostic routine, there is sometimes a need to open connectors, for example to isolate short circuits, which has already been highlighted as undesirable and therefore is minimized.

In addition to component drawings, circuit diagrams etc. Cirrus required a total vehicle electrical system rig to develop the diagnostic hardware and software. This consisted of all the electrical parts of the XJ40, harnesses, sensors, actuators attached to an open wooden framework to allow easy access to connectors etc. Where mechanical stimuli were required to make a system function correctly, for example crankshaft sensor for the engine management system, simulation was provided (see Fig. 6).

However, the vehicle's design was evolving during its development. Cirrus and Jaguar could not develop JDS software with a constantly changing vehicle specification so the concept of a 'frozen' vehicle design was agreed. A rig was built to a fixed design level corresponding to a given date. Software could then be developed by Cirrus for that design level.

Meanwhile all changes to vehicle design that would affect the JDS were monitored and Cirrus was updated

Fig. 6 The total electrical system rig

with drawings and parts for their rig, once software for the previous design level had been written. Cirrus were updated twice during the JDS development. This process also provided valuable feedback on the monitoring and updating procedures which are being used to monitor design changes now the car is in production, to ensure that the JDS remains compatible with the vehicle, for example for model year changes.

For a probe-based diagnosis, a complex question and answer (Q and A) structure had to be developed. This enables the JDS, via operator feedback, to exercise the vehicle system, such as window lifts, and by the answers from the operator identify the function(s) at fault. The operator is then 'guided' through a series of electrical measurements on the vehicle using either or both of the probes.

For a pod-based diagnosis the Q and A phase is much reduced. The operator installs the appropriate 'pod' in the vehicle. The JDS then controls that subsystem itself with minimal intervention from the operator, overriding sensor inputs, isolating or driving outputs. Only if there is a fault in the harness or remote sensors does the JDS tell the operator to use the probes in a 'guided' routine.

The JDS then reaches a diagnosis and displays the fault description to the operator. The printer provides hard-copy output containing information on the fault type, diagnostic route followed, measurements made, date etc. which is returned to Jaguar as a source of design and quality feedback.

After defining the JDS hardware and the methods of visibility and control using the vehicle electrical system and within the above constraints, the diagnostic software was developed.

11 SOFTWARE LANGUAGES

As the 2610-based system processor is an execute only machine and not a development machine, software development work was done on another processor using the following languages:

1. 'C' is a high level programming language compiled to run on the Z80 microprocessor. This is used to control the JDS hardware, I/O and probe drive circuitry. It also handles database retrieval and the 2610 systems, for example disc drive control.
2. GR-PAL is a sub-set of 'C' used directly by the 2610. It is an interpreted language, used to drive the pod-based diagnoses, perform arithmetic functions, screen displays and the question and answer routines in the probe-based systems.
3. TLI (test language interpreter) is a language specially developed for the JDS project. It is based on assembler code and is used when going through a 'guided' probe routine to trace a fault in the vehicle harness. It is called by GR-PAL like a sub-routine and is a compact way of defining:
   (a) which connector is to be probed,
   (b) which screen display is to be used,
   (c) what test limits of the measurement are to be taken,
   (d) what the next step is, dependent on the result of the measurement taken.

Thus software techniques were both complex and extensive but ideally suited for their intended purpose. All vehicle-specific information was then arranged in the following sequence of databases:

Connector information
Graphics panels
Operator questions
Operator messages
Fault codes/descriptions
TLI routines
PAL routines

For example connector information contains:

(a) every connector type, colour and location on the vehicle,
(b) the terminal numbers and corresponding wire colours for every connector.

A graphics package was developed to allow the JDS to display visually:

(a) the location of each connector,
(b) the shape of the connector,
(c) how to probe the connector.

All this is retained in the graphics panels database. Typical screens of information for the operator during a diagnosis are shown in Figs 7 and 8.

The databases were structured with language translation in mind. The text displayed on the JDS screen is available in any one of the following languages:

English
French
German
Italian
Spanish
Dutch

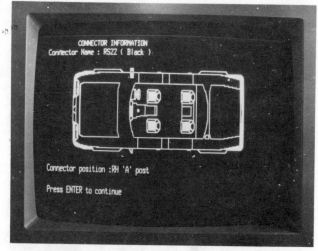

Fig. 7 Graphics screen: vehicle plan view

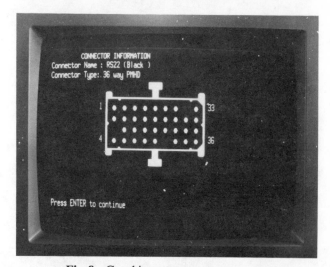

Fig. 8 Graphics screen: connector type

12 OTHER FEATURES

Great effort has been put into making the system easy and attractive to use, an example of this being the measurement probe.

Apart from probe tip illumination to aid probing in dark areas of the vehicle, it has two 'contact-confirmed' LEDs. These help the operator when probing the back of sealed or awkward connectors where visual confirmation that electrical contact with the terminal in the connector has been made. The signals given by LEDs are as follows:

1. When a probing is required, the tip illumination is switched on, the LEDs are flashed at a slow rate and a bias voltage is applied to the tip by the JDS.
2. When the tip makes contact with the connector terminal the bias voltage changes. The JDS senses this and the LEDs are turned off.
3. When the 'M' key is pressed the JDS takes a measurement of the voltage/resistance on the terminal without the bias voltage.
   (a) The LED will come on continuously if the measurement taken is within test limits.
   (b) The LED will flash at a faster rate than before the M key is pressed if the measurement is outside the test limits.

If the operator is happy that he or she made a 'good' measurement he or she can go on to the next stage in the diagnosis by pressing the '↑' key. If not, the operator has the ability to go back and take the measurment again, by pressing the '↓' key.

Apart from the diagnostic mode, the JDS offers three other modes:

1. The self-test is to make sure that the JDS itself is performing correctly before performing a diagnosis.
2. In the multimeter mode the JDS can use its probes as a multimeter to measure voltage, current and resistance.
3. Connector information gives details on connector location colour, type and pin/wire colour information.

While Cirrus developed software on their rig Jaguar undertook to validate and debug the software on vehicles, for example, to take into account the differences in measurements due to alternator output if the engine is required to run, earthing through the bodyshell, component accessibility etc. As problems have arisen these have been fed back to Cirrus who have modified the software which was then checked to ensure that the problems had been resolved. This procedure will be extended to cover any problems encountered in the field.

13 CONCLUSION

Jaguar and GenRad have developed a unique aid to dealers in the franchise which provides:

(a) Common skill levels in all dealerships.
(b) Ease of update through the supply of latest software on a floppy disc.
(c) A high level of certainty in diagnosing potentially complex faults accurately and efficiently.
(d) A test station able to supply a long-term solution to diagnosis, taking account of the company's long-term model plan.

The development of a high comfort, high stability rear suspension

A J Cartwright, BSc
Jaguar Cars Limited, Coventry

Current rear suspension designs for rear-wheel drive high performance luxury vehicles are compromised by the conflicting requirements of handling, stability and passenger comfort. This paper describes the philosophy and development behind the new Jaguar XJ40 independent rear suspension systems and shows that by simple design these compromises can be significantly reduced.

1 INTRODUCTION

In the design of suspensions for passenger vehicles there is a multitude of apparently conflicting objectives towards which the designer struggles to progress:

Good ride quality
Good noise isolation
Low cost
Low weight
High cornering power
Good handling
Good packaging
Ease of assembly
Low maintenance
Reliability
Durability
High ground clearance
etc.

For a high performance luxury car there are three against which there can be no compromise:

1. *Isolation.* The occupants must be provided with an environment which promotes comfort, relaxation and freedom from fatigue. This requires the ultimate in isolation from road disturbances, road noises, power unit noise and vibration, axle noise etc.
2. *Safe handling.* The driver must be provided with a totally predictable vehicle with fast yet controlled responses, high levels of cornering power with progressive limit behaviour, and stable transient behaviour (lane change, lift-off etc). Above all the vehicle must be totally manageable by the non-skilled driver.
3. *Durability and reliability.* Customer expectations of vehicle life, particularly in the luxury sector, are always increasing.

If we explore these further then a number of constant factors will emerge.

2 ISOLATION

Optimum isolation requires a complete understanding of all the noise and vibration paths which lead to the vehicle occupants. In general, however, the overall performance will depend on a number of factors:

(a) Body transfer mobilities, that is the noise and vibration responses at the occupant positions for a force input at the suspension mounting points.
(b) The suspension system transfer functions, that is the net isolation offered by the suspension to road, power unit and internally generated disturbances, in respect of vibration and airborne noise transmission.
(c) The level of disturbance created by the main sources, that is tyre ride and noise qualities, axle gear noise performance and power unit torsional vibration levels.

For the purposes of this paper attention is focused on the transfer functions of the suspension, but brief references on body and tyre performance are contained in references (1) and (2) respectively. Power unit vibration and axle noise performance are outside the scope of this paper.

Basic isolation is provided in any system by interposing some form of spring between the input and the output. This will provide a resonant system which provides attenuation above the resonant frequency but will need damping to ensure manageable amplitudes at resonance. Better isolation is provided if additional mass/spring systems are interposed in series with the main system. Clearly extra resonances are also created, but even with the necessary damping there will be significant advantages in attenuation above resonance.

Most vehicles utilize the 'single'-degree-of-freedom system in the vertical (ride) sense, (that is unsprung mass and roadspring) with varying degrees of success. However, it is clear that in an independently sprung suspension system there will be a significant mass available, in the form of axle and/or sub-frame, which can be utilized to create a two-degree-of-freedom system. The level of isolation will be dependent on the mounted frequency of this part. It is therefore very important that the effective inertia of this system is utilized to its maximum effect and that the softest possible mountings are incorporated.

In the fore and aft sense, somewhat ambiguously referred to as the compliance direction, a similar description is possible. Again most vehicles utilize a single-degree-of-freedom system (unsprung mass and bushes), but in general the designs prevent the use of a very low resonant frequency due to the soft bushes that would be required and the resultant poor geometry control.

As with the ride sense, axles and subframes can be used to advantage by creating a two-degree-of-freedom system, but again the inertias should be used to their best effect.

3 HANDLING

The handling behaviour of a high performance car will depend on many factors, not the least of which is the tyre. However, as far as the rear suspension is concerned there are a number of fundamentals which must not be ignored.

First and foremost good geometric alignment must be maintained under all conditions (bump, rebound, power on/off, cornering etc.). Control over steered angle is the most important and, although very small amounts of throttle or bump steer can be used to advantage in some circumstances, it is best to eliminate parasitic steer angle variations totally. Corner force steer can be used to add further understeer, and hence increase transient response, but will have no effect on ultimate cornering potential. Camber changes are less important but excessive camber angles or rates of change of camber should be avoided. High camber angles give rise to poor tyre wear, and will degrade the tyre's high-speed capability by local overheating in the more heavily loaded shoulder area.

Some compensation for roll angle is useful in steady state cornering conditions but over bumpy or undulating surfaces changes in camber angle are more likely to give rise to poor directional stability. Furthermore, high rates of change of camber will generate torques in the steer sense due to gyroscopic effects. At wheel bounce frequencies the effective coupling between bounce and steer directions will be significant and will present a further refinement problem.

For good handling on non-uniform surfaces tyre contact patch force must be maintained as constant as possible. Simple dynamic considerations show that this dictates a fully independent suspension system and also requires the lowest possible unsprung–sprung mass ratio.

4 DESIGN RULES

It is clear, therefore, that for good refinement and good handling, a number of design rules have emerged:

1. Suspension must be fully independent.
2. Use major masses effectively as part of the isolation system.
3. Use the lowest possible resonant frequency systems.
4. Eliminate parasitic steer angles.
5. Avoid large camber angles.
6. Minimize camber rate of change.
7. Low unsprung mass.

It is interesting, however, to examine the current state-of-the-art rear-wheel drive rear suspension designs in comparison with these guidelines, and there are probably only two basic designs.

4.1 Semi/trailing arm suspension

This arrangement is generally attractive for packaging reasons but it has a number of fundamental deficiencies. Firstly, it has large changes in camber and steer angle with wheel travel and, secondly, if the wishbone bushes are made soft enough to obtain benefit from the primary compliance system then significant throttle steer will be perceived. If the additional problem of squat and lift is considered with this type of suspension then it will be seen that there is inherent difficulty in ensuring optimal transient handling.

Attempts have been made to improve the torque-induced steer (3) with some success, but significant complication is added for small returns in compliance improvement. It is also to be expected that in order to keep camber angles in a reasonable range that somewhat stiffer springing or damping than would otherwise be chosen has to be applied (self-levelling suspension will assist in the steady state).

The pro-squat and lift tendency is also a comfort problem. Lift due to brake torque can again be overcome with complex linkages but the squat problem can only be overcome by stiffer springs and/or dampers which again further compromise comfort.

4.2 Double link suspension

There are many ways of accomplishing this classic layout and it does provide a number of basically helpful features:

(a) total flexibility in terms of geometry and geometry changes with wheel travel,
(b) possibility of full compensation for squat and lift,
(c) relatively low unsprung mass.

It is used fairly successfully in a number of luxury cars and most sports cars. The XJ6 uses the driveshaft as the top link. An alternative is a multi-link variation (4) which recognizes the need for good steer and camber control and goes some way to reducing the conflict between this and the achievement of low longitudinal stiffness. However, maximum benefit is undoubtedly restrained by the load limitations of the rubber joints, and a typical first resonant frequency in the longitudinal direction is of the order of 22 Hz. This is not low enough to be of significant benefit.

It is apparent that nobody currently achieves the very low compliance frequencies necessary to make substantial improvements in comfort and refinement.

5 EARLY DEVELOPMENTS

Against this background it was clear at the start of the XJ40 project that although the current XJ6 suspension performed reasonably well, a number of fundamental changes were required in order to make significant steps forward in refinement.

1. Introduce a primary longitudinal compliance system without compromising geometric alignment.
2. Introduce an anti-squat geometry.

In order to explore all possibilities many ideas were tabled and many prototypes constructed. The following describes a number of the early developments prior to the hard design being laid down.

5.1 Watts linkage

The current Jaguar rear suspension employs a forward facing radius arm to assist in control of pitch and yaw of the unsprung mass and subframe assembly. However, the positioning of this link is contrary to the requirements for anti-squat or anti-lift suspensions, as were the angles of the lower wishbone fulcrum shafts. An early development inclined the wishbone fulcrums to promote anti-squat but the resultant path locus of the hub with wheel travel was incompatible with a simple horizontal radius arm.

To accommodate this it was necessary to install a relatively complex mechanism in the form of a classic Watts linkage, fore and aft at each hub (Fig. 1).

This arrangement gave good geometric control, together with anti-squat, but resulted in no change in terms of compliance systems. Being relatively complex and offering only anti-squat this relatively straightforward development of the current suspension was ruled out.

5.2 IRS 3

A more radical solution was explored in a design affectionately named IRS 3 (Fig. 2). Anti-squat was included by wishbone inclination and radius arms were replaced with controlling 'A' brackets mounted on axes parallel to the wishbones. In this arrangement a secondary isolation system was also included for the axle in order to reduce axle noise transmission, and self-levelling hydraulic damper units were incorporated for further comfort improvements.

Although this design showed much promise, it did not feature a significant improvement in the compliance system, and its design was heavily dependent on the long-nosed two-speed axle casing. When this feature was shelved, the overall design for this arrangement became less attractive.

5.3 Compliant wishbone

An early experiment into low-frequency compliance systems was a system for hub compliance using a wishbone with rotational flexibility (5). The concept was based upon the principle of using the hub carrier as an inverted pendulum. Clearly if the hub carrier was mounted on a shaft and allowed to rotate freely in a

Fig. 2 The IRS 3

vehicle transverse axis through the centre of the lower wishbone, then static loads would constrain the system geometry but a very low stiffness would be presented at the hub centre-line in the compliance direction. Furthermore, there would be a progressively increasing stiffness with wheel movement in the compliance direction in either sense and the system would be inherently stable (Fig. 3).

However, the stiffness by this means alone would be zero in its static condition and would undoubtedly allow wheel movements of excessive amplitude. In order to add stiffness and reduce complexity the pivot axis was provided by a number of tubular rubber elements sandwiched between two coaxial tubes.

The refinement with this system was exceptional, maintaining unsprung mass resonant frequencies in the fore and aft sense lower than those in the vertical sense (wheel bounce).

Further analysis and testing, however, showed that this system had an inherent bump steer problem. Since the rotational axis of the hub carrier was carried in the lower wishbone whenever the wishbone was in a position other than horizontal, hub compliance (that is rotation of the hub carrier) caused a corresponding rotational component in the steer plane, proportional to a function of wishbone and hub inclinations.

It was with great disappointment that this too was shelved.

5.4 Outboard brakes

Although in apparent conflict with the 'golden rule' relating to unsprung mass, it was desired to move away from the current philosophy of inboard, axle-mounted

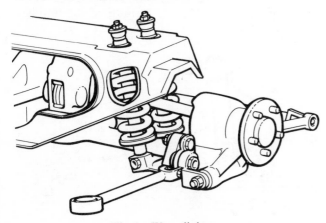

Fig. 1 Watts linkage

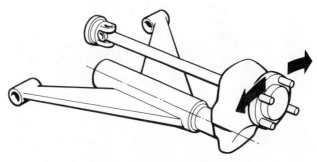

Fig. 3 Compliant wishbone

Fig. 4   Outboard brakes

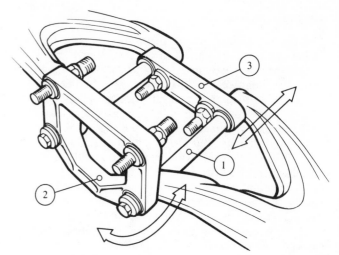

Fig. 6   Diagrammatic of the compliance

brakes in order to improve performance and service-ability. An early experiment remounted the brakes on the hub carriers and included a linkage to provide anti-lift to varying degrees (Fig. 4). Somewhat surprisingly the results showed slight reductions in harshness and better shake control, while showing no perceived deterioration in handling behaviour.

Clearly by moving the mass outboard not only was the wheel bounce frequency reduced but also the suspension yaw resonant frequency—effectively the one wheel compliance frequency. It was also interesting to note that lift produced by rear wheel brake forces was apparently of little significance since total elimination of this showed little improvement in passenger comfort.

Overall this experiment demonstrated the dominance of the compliance system in terms of overall refinement.

5.5 Inboard compliance

The final development continued from the wishbone compliance arrangement. In order to eliminate the steer problem it was very clear that the mechanism of compliance had to be on the sprung side of the suspension (Fig. 5).

The aim therefore was to allow the wishbone and hub assembly to have low fore/aft mounted stiffness while maintaining high stiffness in the lateral direction for good geometric control. Simple rubber bushes of suitable load capacity have stiffness ratios (radial to axial) which are much too low. An arrangement was designed which utilized the high radial rates of relatively conventional bushes to achieve the required lateral stiffness, but which achieved very low fore/aft stiffness through the low conical rates of the bushes (Fig. 6).

The wishbone inner fulcrum (1) was mounted in a pendulum arrangement at the front (2) and a cross tie arrangement (3) at the rear (see Figs 6 and 7). The lateral stiffness of the pendulum is proportional to its width–height ratio and the radial stiffness of the bushes. The fore/aft stiffness is proportional to its height and the conical stiffness of the bushes. For this reason fore/aft and lateral stiffnesses are reasonably independent and a very high ratio can be achieved (6). In fact for an adequate lateral stiffness the fore/aft stiffness is significantly lower than that required for the ideal resonant frequency.

The rear tie design is such that for fore/aft considerations each pair of bushes are in series and hence have low stiffness in total. For accelerating or braking conditions, when high lateral leads are seen in both wishbones, then only the outer bush radial stiffnesses are seen by the wishbone and a high lateral rate is maintained.

During the development phase, an additional resonant mode was discovered in the form of an anti-phase

Fig. 5   Inboard compliance

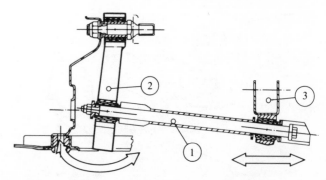

Fig. 7   Schematic of the compliance

coupling between the two wishbones. Modal analysis showed that, to reduce the magnitude of this resonance to an acceptable level, it would be necessary to increase the longitudinal stiffness of the inner bushes by a significant amount. This was most readily achieved by the use of external buffering and, although the basic compliance stiffness was increased, the prime resonant frequency was maintained at a satisfactory low level.

This arrangement performed well, showing improvements in ride comfort, harshness and road noise transmission, and had no side effects in terms of handling behaviour. This would become the backbone of the XJ40 suspension.

6 THE XJ40 REAR SUSPENSION

During the course of these experiments it became very clear that in order to achieve the levels of refinement and handling which the company believed to be necessary for a high performance luxury car then the design would need to start from a clean sheet of paper. For this reason the XJ40 rear suspension contains no carry-over parts from the XJ6.

At the heart of the suspension is the axle assembly (see Fig. 8). The casing for this provides the mounting points for the subframe and compliance system, the rear being through the finned aluminium cover. The pendulum for the compliance system sits astride the axle nose and carries the front end of the inner fulcrum shafts at its lower end. The rear of the inner fulcrum shafts are carried on the rear tie forging, containing the compliance bushes and control buffering, and fixed to the rear of the axle through the inner mounts.

Broad-based pressed steel wishbones form the lower links of the suspension and carry all vertical and fore/aft loadings. The upper link is provided by the driveshaft utilizing conventional Hookes' joints. The hub carrier is in cast aluminium and carries the disc brake caliper and drum parking brake backplate.

The main subframe is attached to the axle casing in four areas and takes the main suspension loads outboard to the body structure main longitudinals and is the main structural component. It comprises pressed steel lower and upper assemblies plus tubular tie bars from the main mountings to the upper face of the axle.

Suspension pitch control is provided by a pair of links at the rear from the rear tie to, again, the body structure main longitudinals.

Spring damper assemblies (combined with a levelling

Fig. 8 Rear suspension

system as required) are fitted between the wishbone and the body structure.

6.1 Suspension geometry

The design of the XJ40 suspension provides a low and relatively stable roll centre and gives small changes of camber with wheel travel. At design condition the camber change rate is low and this, particularly when combined with the suspension levelling height control, gives the rear tyres their optimum conditions for handling, wear and high-speed performance.

The inclined inner wishbone fulcrum provides 50 per cent anti-squat compensation and is combined with a complementary inclination of the outer fulcrum to ensure bump steer is eliminated.

6.2 Mounting system statics

Statically, the positioning of the spring damper unit provides a system whereby all the suspension loads are carried by the front mountings. Similarly, in traction or braking the use of links at the rear again ensures that all the quasi-static forces are handled by the front mounts. This enables the use of a relatively simple subframe and ensures that major loads can be fed into the best point in the body structure. Additionally, since with this arrangement increased loads at the wheel cause the subframe to displace downwards, some compensation for wind-up under acceleration is achieved by virtue of vehicle rearward weight transfer. For this reason mountings of a lower than normal stiffness can be utilized.

The use of an inclined pair of links at the rear provides the additional control required for wind-up, ensures dynamic loads are fed into a point on the structure with low mobility and provides an effective mounting centre at a similar height to the front mounts. This latter point ensures that under conditions of lateral weight transfer steer effects from the subframe are eliminated.

Similarly, by careful selection of mounting stiffnesses in the lateral sense it is possible to ensure that there are no parasitic steer effects generated by applied cornering force. Overall therefore all unwanted steer effects have been eliminated to ensure good straight line stability, optimized geometry for efficient tyre performance and high levels of stability in transient power on/power off conditions.

6.3 Mounting system dynamics

From a refinement aspect, the heart of the system is the longitudinal compliance provided by the pendulum and rear tie system. This provides an isolation system with a very low resonant frequency and hence gives very effective isolation from about 20 Hz upwards. Additionally, the axle and subframe assembly forms the second isolation system providing significant gains in isolation from about 30 Hz and above.

Very careful optimization of the mounting stiffnesses is required, particularly in the vertical sense, in order to ensure that the major resonant modes are sufficiently well separated and are provided with sufficient damping. Close co-operation with the mounting manufacturers has been essential in order to select the most suitable rubber compound for the delicate balance between dynamic stiffness, damping and durability. However, with the design of the XJ40 suspension many of the traditional compromises have been removed by the deliberate elimination of the mounting system directional dependencies, giving the greatest flexibility in choice of stiffness, and a very high level of isolation has been achieved while maintaining good performance in the low-speed ride and shake regions.

The final attachment point to the body is through the spring damper assembly. Theoretically the isolation provided by such a unit will be very good except at the spring resonant frequency and provided the friction in the system is very low. To ensure low friction, low piston and rod guide loads are maintained through the use of a ball-type joint at the lower fixing and the piston and guides themselves have PTFE coatings. The spring resonance is damped by mounting the spring at its upper end on a microcellular polyurethane ring. This material was chosen for its special non-linear stiffness properties, allowing low stiffness at high pre-loads, and for its inherent good damping properties.

7 PERFORMANCE ACHIEVEMENTS

Clearly there are many different analysis techniques for evaluating the dynamic performance of motor vehicles. It is also difficult to demonstrate the performance of the rear suspension alone since it is obviously only one part of a very complex system. However, the results of a number of tests from our standard test programme are included in this paper and in simple terms demonstrate the levels of achievement for the XJ40:

Bump steer	Fig. 9
Bump camber	Fig. 10
Torque steer	Fig. 11
Lift-off oversteer	Fig. 12
Low-speed ride	Table 1

For comparison two typical competitors are included in the results:

Car A	Semi-trailing suspension
Car B	Multi-link suspension

Figures 9 to 11 show basic geometry changes against wheel travel and against tractive effort. The clear advantages of the XJ40 suspension are easily seen giving:

(a) low levels of bump steer,
(b) low levels of camber change,
(c) low levels of throttle steer.

In overall vehicle terms these advantages are most readily demonstrated using a 'lift-off in a turn' test.

The vehicle is driven around a curve of constant radius at a range of constant speeds. At a predetermined point the throttle is quickly released and, with

Table 1 Low-speed ride: mean comfort level in the rear seat at 0–60 km/h

Car	Vertical	Longitudinal
XJ40	0.57	0.39
XJ6	0.68	0.62
A	0.61	0.50
B	0.87	0.54

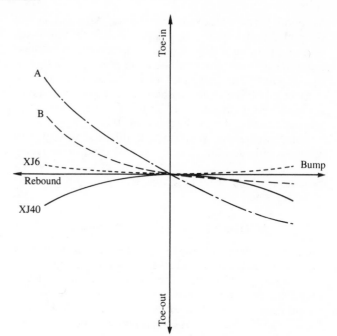

Fig. 9 Bump steer performance

fixed steer control, the resultant vehicle behaviour is subjectively assessed in terms of the amount of apparent oversteer generated. Again it will be seen (Fig. 12) that the stable XJ6 performance is maintained by the XJ40 while the cars with semi-trailing suspension have much less satisfactory performance.

As a simple test for comfort level, the vehicle is mounted on to a rolling road with slats attached to the rollers to provide a standard ride disturbance. Comfort can be measured as manikin accelerations in the vertical and longitudinal directions. Table 1 shows that, while only slight improvements in vertical ride comfort have been achieved with the XJ40 compared to the XJ6, as would be expected, in the fore/aft sense a dramatic improvement is seen. Clearly the 'resultant total comfort' therefore represents a major feature for the XJ40.

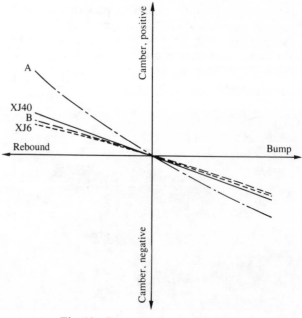

Fig. 10 Bump camber performance

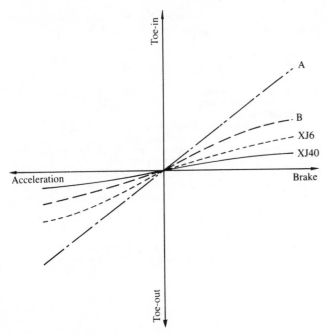

Fig. 11 Torque steer performance

Overall, these simple tests demonstrate that the basic philosophy underlying the XJ40 is fundamentally correct and that exceptional levels of comfort and stability have been achieved.

8 DURABILITY AND RELIABILITY

Good durability and reliability cannot be developed. They are achieved through sound and comprehensive design practices.

Throughout the XJ40 project, the target has been 150 000 miles of service life, with the exception of a small number of serviceable items. For the rear suspension the only serviceable items are the dampers, brake

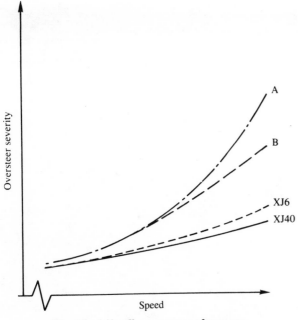

Fig. 12 Lift-off oversteer performance

pads and discs. A major element of the design was to allow easy and rapid changing of these items. The brakes are now outboard with the discs sandwiched between the roadwheel and the hub for easy disc removal. The caliper will pivot away from the disc for easy pad removal. The damper assemblies can be removed by releasing five nuts.

Similarly, should the need arise, the entire rear suspension can be removed by undoing a handful of fixings and services without disturbing the exhaust system. Therefore, for routine and even non-routine maintenance, time in the workshop will be minimized.

8.1 Specifications

The fundamental design philosophy for the XJ40 was such that for every component there would be not only a drawing which described how it should be made but also a comprehensive specification to describe what it has to achieve.

The specification would describe the environment, the life expectations and the specific performance requirements and would detail the rig-based testing which would enable the supplier to guarantee continued reliability.

It also ensured that the component supplier would, no matter how far removed from the vehicle manufacturer, fully understand the environment in which his component had to function—a major but often forgotten point.

8.2 Vehicle testing

The XJ40 is a world specification car. The design concept was such that each component should be suitable for, for example, the −40°C snow conditions of Canada, the +52°C high-humidity conditions in the Middle East, the high-speed driving on German autobahns, the punishing dust and stones of the Australian outback. While many of these conditions can be individually simulated in the laboratory or on the test track, there is currently no total substitute for real environmental testing. For the XJ40, 85 prototypes (plus a large number of simulators) have been tested in many areas of the world for over $5\frac{1}{2}$ million miles. Typical test sites were:

Timmins, Canada
Phoenix, Arizona
Nardo, Italy
Sydney and Cobar, Australia
Oman, Middle East
Coventry, England
New York City

Many lessons have been learnt and design changes incorporated. Final validation took place last winter and during the early part of this year, using off-tool components and vehicles built on the production line.

8.3 Rig testing

From a reliability standpoint, whereas the number of test miles achieved is impressive, the number of test samples (that is vehicles or units) is relatively small. In order to ensure that the highest levels of reliability were attained a major rig test programme was carried out in parallel with the vehicle programme. By this means, large numbers of components could be tested and reliability measured on a sound statistical base.

Road load and stress data were generated where necessary from early prototypes (7) and a suite of rigs were designed and built using these data. Each major system or component was tested in this manner for initial validation, and this testing will continue throughout the vehicle life to ensure that continuing high levels of reliability are maintained for every vehicle produced.

9 CONCLUSIONS

The results of the simple tests shown in this paper, and the experience of over 5 million miles, demonstrate that it is possible to design a rear suspension for a rear-wheel drive luxury car that has virtually no compromises between refinement, handling and durability.

REFERENCES

1 **Dunn, J. W.** and **Brown, A. M.** A dynamic modelling technique for the XJ40 body structure design. *Proc. Instn Mech. Engrs*, Part D, 1986, **200**, this issue.
2 **Day, P., Holmes, T.** and **Major, D.** TD tyres for Jaguar. *Proc. Instn Mech. Engrs.*, Part D, 1986, **200**, this issue.
3 **Matsokinsky, W.** Further developments of the semi trailing arm. *Automobiltechnische Zeitschrift*, 1982, **84**, 7/8.
4 **Enke, K.** Improvement of the ride/handling compromise in the elasto-kinematic system of wheel suspension. IMechE conference, *Road vehicle handling*, May 1983, pp. 91–96 (Mechanical Engineering Publications, London).
5 UK Patent 2059366.
6 UK Patent 2125742.
7 **Tivey, C. J.** The utilization of fatigue life prediction techniques in support of a major vehicle project. *Proc. Instn Mech. Engrs*, Part D, 1986, **200**, this issue.

TD tyres for Jaguar

P S Day, BSc, **T Holmes,** CEng, MRAeS and **D J Major,** BSc, CEng, MIMechE
SP Tyres UK Limited, Fort Dunlop, Birmingham

This paper gives a technical description of the Dunlop 220/65VR390 TD SP Sport D7 safety tyre and wheel and a summary of the testing methods used in its development for the Jaguar XJ40.

Engineers at SP Tyres knew from their long and close association with Jaguar that the XJ40 represented a major advance in the luxury/high performance sector of the market. It is believed that the tyre which has been developed and homologated is a significant advance in the field of tyre technology.

To obtain the required handling and steering properties to complement the XJ40, it was necessary to adopt a 65 per cent aspect ratio (see Fig. 1). Good vehicle handling is achieved when the tyre forces and response levels generated are sufficiently high to resist the forces created by the vehicle during any transient or steady state limit manoeuvre (see Appendix 1). To provide other advances in performance the tyre size selected was 220/65VR390 TD, which meant the design of a special wheel.

The slight disadvantage of selecting a 65 series aspect ratio in place of the 70 series (which has been used so successfully on the Series III model) would have been expected to show as a comfort loss (see Fig. 2). Comfort and ride acceptability is the result of subjective 'blindfold' comparison testing over a fixed circuit of varying road surfaces and over a range of speeds (see Appendix 1).

This potential penalty, however, has been avoided by the adoption of the TD tyre and rim. With a unique TD groove, the tyre bead locates more securely than a standard inch-sized tyre on a standard wheel, thus allowing the rim to have a lower flange height—some 6 mm or one-third lower than for the standard wheel.

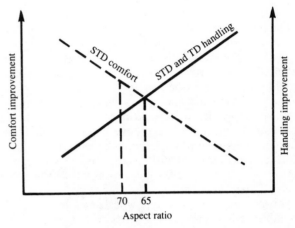

Fig. 2 Effect of aspect ratio on handling and comfort

A lower flange height increases the free sidewall length by the same amount and, therefore, recovers the loss in comfort associated with the shorter sidewall of a 65 series tyre (see Fig. 3).

Such a combination of aspect ratio and TD construction ensures excellent ride comfort with significantly improved handling properties (see Fig. 4).

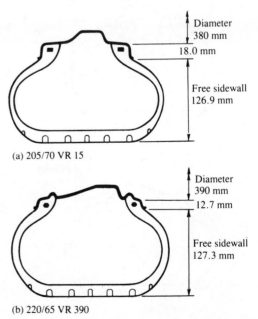

(a) 205/70 VR 15

Diameter
380 mm
18.0 mm
Free sidewall
126.9 mm

Diameter
390 mm
12.7 mm
Free sidewall
127.3 mm

(b) 220/65 VR 390

Fig. 3 Comparison of rim and free sidewall dimensions

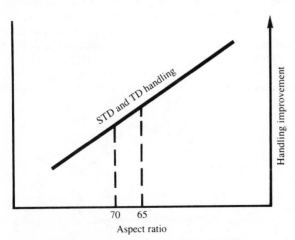

Fig. 1. Effect of aspect ratio on handling

0265-1904/86 $2.00 + .05

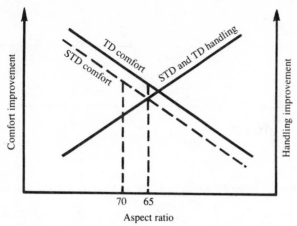

Fig. 4   Recovery of comfort level by adoption of TD

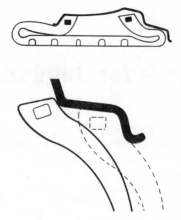

Fig. 6   Standard bead dislodgement

The 390 TD rim offers an increase of some 10 mm in the bead and wheel diameter over the nearest inch equivalent—15 inch. This larger rim diameter gives the potential for improved brakes and/or brake cooling should it be required (see Fig. 5).

The TD tyre incorporates a hexagonal multi-coil bead core together with a bead toe extension, which slots into a corresponding groove in the wheel. These features combine to provide improved torsional rigidity, which enhances the tyre dislodgement performance, preventing dislodgement even down to total deflation (see Figs 6, 7 and Table 1).

This provides the safest tyre/wheel assembly currently available commercially. This safety feature enables the driver of a vehicle which has suffered a sudden deflation to maintain full vehicle control.

The final feature of the TD wheel/tyre assembly offering a distinct advance on standard inch-sized assemblies is the adoption of the Airloc sealant gel which reduces, by up to two-thirds, the chances of suffering a total tyre deflation (see Fig. 8).

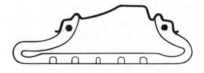

Fig. 7   TD bead retention

Table 1   Dislodgement results (full lock 'J' turn)

Rim	Speed mile/h	Pressure lbf/in^2
STD flat ledge (205/70VR15 D7)	25 tyre dislodged	8
TD (220/65VR390 TD)	25 no dislodgement	0

Even in the case of more extensive damage the incorporation of sealant gel would mean a partial retention of air pressure or at least reduce the rate of air loss. The application of a sealant in a standard inch tyre is not regarded as a safe practice because the tyre is likely to suffer a bead dislodgement at low pressures.

The use of Airloc sealant has been tested and proven over many millions of vehicle miles by the customer in

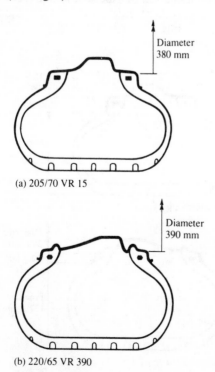

Fig. 5   Brake space comparison

Fig. 8   Location of sealant gel

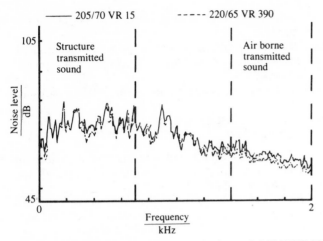

Fig. 9 Noise frequency graph: comparison of 205/70VR15 and 220/65VR390

the development and road proving of the XJ40, including sustained high-speed conditions at the Nardo test track in the South of Italy (see Appendix 2).

All these improvements have resulted from the adoption of metric TD technology in place of the standard inch tyre and wheel.

Dunlop have made a number of further advances on the tyres developed for the XJ40. The well-proven D7 pattern, which was developed around the Series III, has been significantly modified and improved to give the XJ40 an even higher level of refinement. The changes are a reproportioning of the pattern ribs and a deepening of the pattern grooves to maximize the wet grip and handling performance.

By rescrambling the pattern elements, it has been possible to reduce further the tyre-generated noise levels (see Fig. 9 and Appendix 3).

To give the best balance of vehicle handling with good steering response it was necessary to ensure that the rim width exceeded that of the tread, as is the case

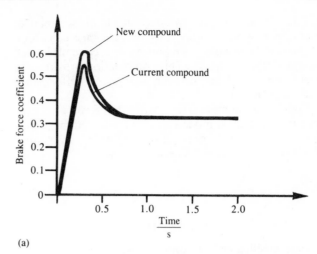

(a)

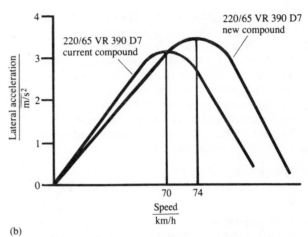

(b)

Fig. 11 Effect of new compound in 220/65VR390 TD (a) on straight ahead braking and (b) on wet grip cornering

with the 220/65VR390 tyre and wheel (see Fig. 10). This is a concept jointly developed by the company and its customer.

An improved tread rubber compound has been incorporated into the tyre which provides some 5 per cent improvement in wet grip performance, both during braking and cornering (see Appendix 4 and Fig. 11). The compound further provides better levels of dry handling performance without any reduction in potential tread life.

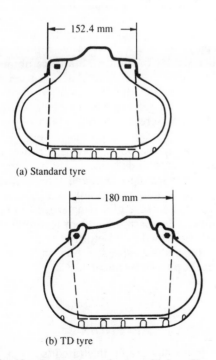

Fig. 10 Comparison of trapezoidal profiles

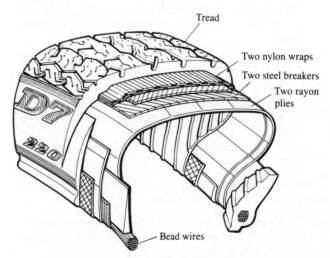

Fig. 12 Cutaway section of 220/65VR390 TD

The construction of the tyre consists of two plies of rayon, plus a tread-supporting belt package consisting of two cut steel layers overlaid by two circumferential, 0° nylon layers (Fig. 12). This combination provides the best possible balance between high-speed performance and ride comfort.

Finally, to achieve even better levels of tyre uniformity, a modified process has been adopted for manufacturing the bead cores using a continuously wound single wire to provide the hexagonal shape.

APPENDIX 1

Vehicle handling and ride comfort tests

To establish the 220/65VR390 TD D7 tyre's suitability for the XJ40 car fitment a number of subjective handling and stability tests were carried out.

These tests were carried out by the vehicle engineers and covered a very wide range of circuit and road conditions. This testing was used to assess the vehicle's ability to return to a stable condition following a cornering, transient and steady state manoeuvre.

The steering behaviour of the vehicle was assessed by the following programme.

(a) *Steering feel*
   On centre feel at 100 km/h with a steering span of 0–60°

(b) *Steering precision*
   Response over the speed range with 0–20° steering
   Aligning torque up to 100 km/h at 30–60° steering
   Aligning torque over 100 km/h at 30–60° steering
   Precision in curves of 0.3 g at 55 km/h; 80 m radius assessment of understeer and/or oversteer
   Precision in curves of 0.7 g at 85 km/h; 80 m radius assessment of understeer and/or oversteer.

(c) *Direction stability*
   Straight ahead running on a level surface road at 110 km/h and above
   Straight ahead running on an undulating surface road at 110 km/h and above
   Bias steering pull to either side over speed range of vehicle
   Throttle steer. Deviation from either straight line or curve due to changes in throttle over the speed range
   Emergency manoeuvre carried out at 110 km/h using 0–90 degrees steer.

(d) *Cornering stability*
   Lateral adhesion. Steady state cornering. Dry grip
   Lane changing. Normal rates of steer over the speed range
   Alternating curves in slalom made over the speed range

The ride/comfort levels of the XJ40 were assessed using the following programme:

(a) *Cushioning* Running over harsh surface and projections at speeds of 50–100 km/h. This is a blindfold subjective test.

(b) *Noise levels* Subject and objective assessment of in-car noise levels over different surfaces at various speeds.

(c) *Drumming* Running over high macrotexture surfaces.

(d) *Tread pattern noise* During acceleration and deceleration.

(e) *Cornering squeal* running over traffic polished surface.

(f) *Uniformity* Assessment of vibration through the steering wheel.

Additional tests on A and B roads take into account such factors as road camber, undulating surfaces and ever-changing surface textures.

The 220/65VR390 TD D7 tyre was proved to have met its objectives, thus complementing the very high standard of handling demanded of the new vehicle.

APPENDIX 2

Tyre sealant

In addition to the extensive sealant gel testing carried out by the customer, the company has operated a test programme over the past five years to assess all aspects of gel sealing capability and any gel movements as a result of high-speed centrifugal effects and high acceleration and decelerations.

The sealing capabilities were assessed from results of testing with police forces in Scotland and North Wales which operated under conditions which gave a high tyre tread penetration level and consequential deflations. The conditions giving this high puncture level were mostly inner city operations covering the patrol of new building sites and slate and stone quarry patrols which contained explosive stores and had to be checked by police cars during the day and throughout the night. These conditions gave a puncture and consequential deflation level which was much higher than that normally experienced in town and urban areas.

The TD tyres were monitored by technical personnel and compared with standard tyres without gel operating under similar conditions. Statistics obtained from these monitored field tests and general surveys on tyres in service showed that the deflation frequency of standard tyres without gel was 1 every 25 000 car miles and is caused by nails, screws or other similar objects.

The TD tyres containing gel sealed some 70 per cent of penetrations at the point that penetration occurred, thus reducing the total deflation factor by some 3 to 1.

During winter testing in Finland tyres containing gel were subjected to internal gel adhesion tests and puncture sealing over a range of driving speeds and distances and at ambient temperatures down to minus 20°C. All tyres tested performed satisfactorily.

The customer's high-speed testing at Nardo covered temperatures up to ambients of 40°C.

APPENDIX 3

The noise frequency graph illustrated (see Fig. 9) is the results of an indoor tyre test on a 1.52 m diameter drum which had a BS594 motorway surface. The tyre was run at a load of 590 kg at a speed of 50 and 80 km/h and also at 100–50 km/h run down in both forward and reverse directions using an operating pressure of 2.35 bar.

The drum surface was a replica of an actual road made up into resin shells which fit on to the drum. The shells have outer layers with silicon carbide filler for high resistance to polishing and give a polished stone value of 58 which is close to the value for granite.

The accuracy of the surface microtexture has been checked by photomicrographs using the scanning electron microscope.

The thermal conductivity of the resin material is close to that of the road and gives typical road tyre temperatures.

The noise levels were picked up from a microphone positioned 450 mm from the ground plane and 800 mm from the centre of contact of the tyre and in the vertical plane containing the drum axle.

The British Standard test for room suitability was used and found to be acceptable. It was found that when the microphone-to-source distance was doubled there was more than a 5 dB drop in sound level in the frequency bands.

A check on the stability of the results showed only after a 0.15 dB(A) drift over a period of one hour after the tyre had reached a stable temperature.

APPENDIX 4

Wet grip vehicle testing

The wet grip testing of the 220/65VR390 TD D7 involved longitudinal wet braking and wet cornering.

The straight ahead braking was carried out on three surfaces, namely Bridport pebble, smooth concrete and smooth asphalt. These different surface textures were used to assess the compound, pattern and construction effects of the tyres. The surfaces were constantly wetted by water sprays which kept the surface water depth to approximately 1 mm. The speed range used for the longitudinal braking was 50–130 km/h and the test results were obtained using an in-car data acquisition system recording deceleration, acceleration and lateral acceleration.

The wet cornering tests used the same equipment set up as for straight ahead braking, again using Bridport pebble and smooth concrete surfaces to differentiate the compound, pattern and construction assessments. To ensure the precise speed of the vehicle, wheel speed pick-ups were incorporated and this, with the known radius of curvature, enabled calculated results to be made. The curvatures used during the cornering tests were 70 m for the smooth concrete and 30 m for Bridport pebble.

From these recorded results the graphs illustrated (see Fig. 11) were drawn.

A dynamic modelling technique for the XJ40 body structure design

A M Brown, PhD and **J W Dunn,** MSc, PhD
Automotive Engineering Centre, Faculty of Mechanical Engineering, University of Birmingham

This paper combines the principles of quantitative structural dynamics standards with a theoretical modelling analysis, and applies it to the Jaguar XJ40 body structure design. This work has resulted in high levels of vehicle refinement in terms of noise and vibration transmitted to the occupant in the complete car.

1 INTRODUCTION

Jaguar Cars have made significant advances in the theoretical and experimental analysis of the motor vehicle system. As a critical component from a vehicle refinement point of view, the body structure has received particular attention. Until recently, the dynamic behaviour has been difficult to characterize theoretically, but the application of finite element methods has brought the problem of analysing such a complex structure within the reach of most vehicle designers. Experience has shown, however, that great care must be taken in using such programmes, particularly in the representation of panel elements and structural damping; otherwise significant differences may be observed between the predicted and final structural dynamic response.

Experimentally, modal analysis of the body structure is now widely used, giving an animated representation of the many vibrational mode shapes. A limited number of problems may be solved in this way, but the major disadvantage is that only a relatively narrow frequency bandwidth can be investigated at a time. An extensive bibliography on such modal analysis techniques is contained in Ewins' exposition of this method (1).

During the programme, however, the introduction and application of structure dynamic performance standards (2, 3) has made it possible to quantify the vehicle structure with respect to noise and vibration over a wide frequency range. Using these techniques, it was possible to decide at an early stage whether or not the XJ40 body structure could finally be built into an acceptable vehicle from a total refinement point of view. The diagnostic and analytical strength of this method is illustrated in this paper, by application to the XJ40 body, and ultimately in the final levels of refinement achieved in the completed car.

As an extension of this approach, the present paper describes a method to derive the vehicle body modal parameters from the dynamic response of the structure. These parameters may then be used to simulate the total response of the body either in isolation or more simply as one part of the total vehicle system.

2 VEHICLE STRUCTURE DYNAMIC PERFORMANCE PARAMETERS

The use of vehicle structural dynamic performance standards in assessing the vehicle body represents a significant departure from traditional methods of assessing the vehicle structure by simply looking at resonant mode shapes, either in the form of mode shape diagrams or animated mode shape displays. The principal advantage of the structural dynamic standards method over the more traditional techniques lies in the fact that it is now possible to assess a vehicle structure in terms of performance figures over a narrow or broad frequency bandwidth, taking into account the integrated effects of all the resonant and non-resonant modes in that bandwidth (2–4).

As a result of this work, quantitative standards have now been set for the dynamic performance of attachment points on the vehicle structure. These are typically for suspension, engine and other running gear, that is point mobility, in addition to the performance of the whole structure itself, or some part of it, with respect to such inputs, that is, modal mobility. These standards have been concluded from extensive testing on a wide variety of vehicle body structures and are set on both a narrowband and broadband basis (5). This takes account of individual modes as well as the integrated effect of many modes. In the case of the XJ40, these standards have been applied so that the dynamic performance of the new vehicle structure was assessed against the dynamic standards for structures in its own class, in addition to the Series III saloon it replaces. A decision could then be made as to its acceptability. This was of particular importance at the prototype stage before extensive commitment to production tooling has been processed.

In the event of an unsatisfactory performance in any area, the diagnostic strength of these methods was shown to be such that the regions of poor performance both in terms of frequency and local structure vibration were identified. Typically, the vibrational energy imbalance between separate panels was exposed, showing that appropriate structural modification would be necessary. Such imbalance of vibrational energy reflects the improper distribution of mass and stiffness among the panels and members of the structure. The need to expose such distribution by the derivation of the modal parameters is clear. In the present case, the mass and stiffness was redistributed for optimum performance of the structure from a refinement point of view.

3 DERIVATION OF VEHICLE MODAL PARAMETERS

The vehicle structure dynamic performance data is determined from experimental tests which are performed using single-point forced vibration testing. The structure is excited at a single point, and frequency responses are measured at a large number of points on the structure. From these measurements, the frequency responses of the input point and a large number of defined elemental areas (up to 70) have been determined. These elemental responses are then vectorially combined to form the averaged frequency response for a smaller number of larger areas. It is from these frequency responses (which are available in both amplitude and phase) that the modal parameters of the structure are determined. The measured data, therefore, are those of an N degrees-of-freedom system, where N is the total number of area frequency responses measured, including that of the input element.

3.1 Theoretical analysis of system

A vehicle is generally a sheet metal structure. A model with hysteretic damping has therefore been selected. Although neither hysteretic or viscous damping is the 'complete' choice—the truth being a mixture of the two—sheet metal structures have been shown to respond closely to a hysteretically damped type of model.

A set of matrices may be defined as $[M]$, $[K]$ and $[H]$, representing respectively the mass, stiffness and hysteretic damping. All these matrices are $N \times N$, and refer to the N areas on the structure which will define the structure's behaviour. The basic model for the vehicle body may be stated as follows:

$$[M][\ddot{x}] + [K][x] + i[H][x] = [F] \tag{1}$$

where

[x] = displacement response matrix
[ẍ] = acceleration response matrix
[F] = forcing function matrix

This is the general equation of motion for the vehicle body system and may be rewritten as

$$[K + iH - \omega^2 M][x] = [F] \tag{2}$$

The equation for free motion is

$$[K + iH - \omega^2 M][x] = 0 \tag{3}$$

This equation has an eigensolution, comprising of a diagonal eigenvalue matrix $[\lambda^2]$ and an eigenvector matrix $[\Psi]$. Both of these are complex, and they give the system's N natural frequencies, modal dampings and mode shapes. The rth eigenvalue λ_r gives both the

natural frequency (ω_r) and the modal damping (η_r) of the rth mode from

$$\lambda_r^2 = \omega_r^2(1 + i\eta_r) \tag{4}$$

The corresponding eigenvector in $[\Psi]$, denoted by $\{\Psi\}_r$, defines the corresponding mode shape. The elements of this vector are complex, and so the mode shape contains phase information as well as magnitude. Because the mode shapes are unscaled, some form of normalization is required, which takes the form of

$$\lceil m_r \rfloor = [\Psi]^T[M][\Psi] \tag{5}$$

$$\lceil k_r \rfloor = [\Psi]^T[K + iH][\Psi] \tag{6}$$

In this work, both m_r and k_r are defined as unity. The above equations concern free vibration, whereas forced excitation is required in the modelling. It may be shown (1) that the harmonic response of a structure may be expressed as the sum of a set of terms containing its modal properties:

$$\frac{\dot{x}_j}{F_k} = \sum_{r=1}^{N} \left[\frac{i\omega \,_r\Psi_j \,_r\Psi_k}{m_r \omega_r^2\{1 - (\omega/\omega_r)^2 + i\eta_r\}} \right] \tag{7}$$

Now, defining a modal flexibility, A, as follows:

$$_rA_{jk} = \frac{_r\Psi_j \,_r\Psi_k}{m_r \omega_r^2} \tag{8}$$

equation (7) becomes

$$\frac{\dot{x}_j}{F_k} = \sum_{r=1}^{N} \left[\frac{i\omega \,_rA_{jk}}{1 - (\omega/\omega_r)^2 + i\eta_r} \right] \tag{9}$$

If all the terms of the eigenvector matrix $[\Psi]$ can be found, and also the values of modal damping and natural frequency, then it is possible to determine all the elements of the mass, stiffness and damping matrices. Normalization and rearrangement of equations (5) and (6) give

$$[M] = [\Phi]^{T^{-1}}[\Phi]^{-1} \tag{10}$$

$$[K + iH] = [\Phi]^{T^{-1}}[\lambda][\Phi]^{-1} \tag{11}$$

where $[\Phi]$ is the normalized eigenvector matrix.

3.2 Determination of modal constants

The method used to determine the modal constants is governed by two distinct criteria, viz. the characteristics of the dynamic system and the techniques used to acquire the experimental data. The dynamic responses of vehicle bodies are characterized by systems with very low damping and loosely separated modes. These two factors indicate that a simple analysis technique could be adequate to determine the modal characteristics. With the XJ40 development, the application of single sine excitation and a frequency response analyser have given exceptional dynamic response accuracy in terms of both amplitude and phase throughout the frequency range, including off-resonant frequencies. The analysis described here has been derived to make full use of these factors, while keeping the method as simple as possible.

Because the body modes are loosely coupled, it is assumed that in the region of any one mode, the contribution from all the other modes is constant. Further, low damping values will provide responses that approximate to a circle, thus giving ideal conditions for a single-degree-of-freedom type of analysis. In the region of any mode the phase angle for any mode given by equation (9) becomes

$$\alpha = \tan^{-1} \frac{1 - (\omega/\omega_r)^2}{\eta_r} \qquad (12)$$

Considering a set of n experimental points in the region of this mode, the total squared error in phase change between each successive pair of points (θ, θ_{i+1}) is

$$\sum \text{Error}^2 = \sum_{i=1}^{n-1} \left[\tan^{-1} \frac{1 - (\omega_i/\omega_r)^2}{\eta_r} - \tan^{-1} \frac{1 - (\omega_{i+1}/\omega_r)^2}{\eta_r} - \theta_i + \theta_{i+1} \right]^2 \qquad (13)$$

The true values of modal constants for the mode will minimize the squared error term in equation (13). The values of ω_r and η_r which minimize the square error must be found. The method adopted here uses the first partial derivatives of equation (13) with respect to both the natural frequency and modal damping values. The derivatives are numerically calculated, since direct integration of equation (13) makes the solution unduly complex, and a simple iterative method is then used to find the minimum solution, generally converging in under ten seconds. Although a more complex algorithm to minimize the equation could have been used, with a possible increase in speed, it was considered more important to retain the ability to perform the analysis using a modest computer facility.

The frequency and modal damping are therefore now known for each mode, the only unknown in equation (9) being the modal flexibility A. If we now set

$$B = \frac{i\omega}{1 - (\omega/\omega_r)^2 + i\eta_r} \qquad (14)$$

this is now known, and so equation (9) may be rewritten as

$$\frac{\dot{x}}{F} = \sum_{i=1}^{n} {}_iA_j \, {}_kB_i \qquad (15)$$

This forms a set of n linear simultaneous equations in ${}_iA_{jk}$, and so a simple matrix solution may be used to determine the full set of modal flexibilities. Hence, the distributed mass, stiffness and damping matrices may now be evaluated, using equations (8), (10) and (11).

4 THE SEPARATION OF COUPLED MODES

Although one of the primary observations stated earlier that vehicle structure dynamic responses were typically composed of loosely coupled modes, the technique described here is also valid and suitable for separating modes with a considerable degree of coupling, provided that the damping level is sufficiently low. The method used for the estimation of the modal parameters does not require data at the resonant condition. The overall important criterion is that there are data of high integration from the off-resonant region either above or below the resonance.

To identify a coupled pair of modes, two segments of

the response are used, one on each side of the region containing the resonant condition. It is then possible to extract the modal constants for each mode individually. This has implications in other areas, as it is sometimes undesirable to excite a very lightly damped structure at its resonant condition. By using single sine excitation, the area close to the resonance may be avoided in the frequency sweep, but the response through the resonance may be determined from the modal constants.

5 THEORETICALLY EXCITED MODEL EXAMPLE

One example of the results from the above technique is applied to the XJ40 structure and is shown in Figs 1 and 2. This shows the experimental point mobility curve, together with the theoretically obtained response. The accuracy of the theoretical response shows how the relatively simple model can characterize such a complex vehicle structure. The theoretical transfer mobilities have been predicted in the same way, and with similar accuracy.

6 SUMMARY AND CONCLUSIONS

Jaguar Cars, in co-operation with the Automotive Engineering Centre at the University of Birmingham, has in recent years developed quantitative structural dynamic analysis techniques which use the modal mobility function to determine the characteristics of vehicle body structures. These techniques have been applied to the XJ40 development programme, and have made a significant contribution to the achievement of the exceptionally low levels of vibration and internally

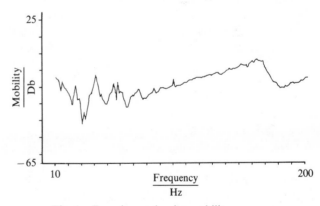

Fig. 1 Experimental point mobility response

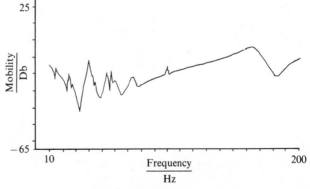

Fig. 2 Theoretical point mobility response

generated noise. Based on this work, the present paper describes a new theoretical modelling extension which, being fully compatible with the earlier experimental techniques, further enhances their original usefulness.

The theoretical analysis is attractive in its simplicity, and is based on the application of single-degree-of-freedom techniques to the full multi-mode response, which is typical of a vehicle body structure. The evaluation of the modal parameters is fast, and has been designed to make full use of the exceptional off-resonant accuracy of single sine forcing to such vehicle systems. The quality of the test data is very high, and has therefore allowed a relatively simple algorithm to be performed quickly on a small computer system. The analysis is not restricted to resonant data, but is equally powerful applied to off-resonant information in allowing coupled modes to be separated. The analysis leads to the distributed spring, mass, damper system representation, and provides for theoretical system excitation and subsequent recovery of the theoretical modal mobility function. The total approach is therefore directly compatible with the earlier developed experimental modal mobility techniques.

REFERENCES

1 **Ewins, D. J.** Whys and wherefores of modal testing. Report 78005, 1978, Dynamics Section, Mechanical Engineering, Imperial College, London.

2 **Dunn, J. W., Olatunbosun, O. A.** and **Mills, B.** Standardisation techniques for the dynamic performance of monocoque vehicle structures. Institute of Measurement and Control Symposium on *Dynamic analysis of vehicle ride and manoeuvering characteristics*, London, 28–30 November 1978, pp. 167–177.

3 **Dunn, J. W., Olatunbosun, O. A.** and **Mills, B.** A diagnostic vibration and acoustic performance analysis of monocoque vehicle structures. *Inst. Acoustics Proc.*, 1979, **20**, paper B3.

4 **Dunn, J. W., Olatunbosun, O. A., El-Seoud, S. A.** and **Mills, B.** 1979, The application of dynamic performance standards in the design and development of a case study prototype structure. *Proc. Nauka I Motorna Vozila* (*Science and Motor Vehicles*), Yugoslav Society of Automotive Engineers, 1979, **3**, 116–131.

5 **Dunn, J. W., Olatunbosun, O. A.** and **Mills, B.** Realistic prediction and control of vehicle noise resulting from road inputs. ASME paper 79-DET-75, 1979.

The design and assessment of the XJ40 instruments and controls

C Holtum
Jaguar Cars Limited, Coventry

The process of designing new vehicle instruments and controls is discussed together with the ergonomic work undertaken to ensure the successful integration of these new features with existing systems in the Jaguar XJ40.

1 INTRODUCTION

As concept studies were carried out for the XJ40, it became apparent that consideration should be taken of the advantages offered in the developing trends in electronic displays. The company's traditional requirement of a high level of accurate instrumentation coupled with a conservative but tasteful styling theme needed to be married to the many advantages available in reliability, accuracy and cost effectiveness of modern instrument technology.

One advantage of the new technology was the flexibility of systems, thus enabling many functions to be incorporated into single areas in positions of optimum use to the driver. This is demonstrated by the application of technology to create a display which will rapidly and effectively alert the driver when any malfunction occurs.

In recent years the number of warning functions displayed in cars has grown rapidly, many of them mandatory requirements associated with safety and emission control systems. Traditionally, these have been single areas dedicated to specific warning functions with the consequence that manufacturers have found it difficult, time consuming and costly to respond to legislative changes or market variations. The introduction of international symbol standards has alleviated this problem, but packaging constraints and design flexibility requirements challenged the company to find new answers to these difficulties. As a result, an information display has been developed as part of the overall instrument package which was to be microprocessor-driven and would provide a single area displaying ISO-based symbols supplemented by an alphanumeric readout (Fig. 1).

The initial product brief for the XJ40 required an evaluation of the potential for a trip computer in the vehicle. Account was taken of problems inherent in those already being offered in cars and whether they were passing gimmicks or out of character with the product. As a result it was decided to integrate a driver-addressable system into the overall design, and the development of the keyboard and displays started.

The company has always considered driver comfort an important contributing factor to the accurate and safe control of its vehicles. Air conditioning has become almost the norm in many markets in the world and the new electronic technologies have widened the scope for the improvement of the function and features of this system. The detailed design and development of the air conditioning package is the subject of a companion publication to this. This paper will limit itself to the work carried out to design the driver air conditioning controls and the subsequent ergonomic studies used to refine that design.

In a highly specified, modern car the introduction of more new features must be carefully analysed to ensure they form a harmonious ergonomic system with all the other controls and displays already in the vehicle. As the XJ40 developed, this became one of the main priorities and considerable design effort and ergonomic evaluation has been undertaken to refine the car to the current high levels of instrumentation. The instrumentation enables the driver to gain ready access to information and easily input control functions without detracting from the primary task of driving the vehicle safely.

Fig. 1 Vehicle condition monitor (VCM)

0265-1904/86 $2.00 + .05

All the normal avenues of design review were available and used in reaching the final layout of controls and displays for the vehicle. These include:

1. In-house experience and market feedback
2. Trends that the competition were setting
3. The mass of information being provided by various potential suppliers
4. In-house testing and evaluation of various systems
5. An independent evaluation of various systems that were proposed

The use of an independent outside organization to validate the work was considered of prime importance when one realizes that it is very easy to convince oneself that one has created an improved system and yet to be blinkered as to how the control or display will actually perform when used by the customer. Comment was therefore sought from the Institute for Consumer Ergonomics Automotive Ergonomics Unit at Loughborough during 1981 and Jaguar subsequently embarked upon a joint programme to tune and validate the designs by means of further research coupled with consumer testing.

The research programme with the Institute covered the following areas:

1. An ergonomic assessment of the instrumentation
2. The design and evaluation of the vehicle condition monitor display
3. The design and evaluation of the trip computer
4. The design and evaluation of the environmental controls

2 AN ERGONOMIC EVALUATION OF THE INSTRUMENTATION

Design of the instrument panel was well progressed by the time the Institute was asked for comments. It had already been decided not to go completely digital with its instrument display but to maintain the traditional use of large speedometer and tachometer analogue dials coupled with the four minor gauges (Fig. 2). Review of the instrument technologies available at that time brought about the decision to use vacuum fluorescent displays as a reliable system for the minor gauges, together with other associated warning function displays. This has given a good blend of traditional and modern displays which together have enhanced the instrumentation of the vehicle.

Fig. 2   The instrument panel

A well-documented basis existed for the designs of the large instruments and ergonomic advice was directed towards the graphic style, chaplet layout, pointer design and effects of coloured backlighting to match the analogue dials to the fluorescent gauges (**1, 2**). One design feature pioneered was the use of a secondary digital speedometer to carry the necessary alternative metric/imperial speed reference. It is a mandatory requirement for all UK vehicles to carry a kilometric scale as well as the normal miles per hour, and the use of the secondary display has led to a less cluttered, easier to read main speedometer dial. The advantage to the driver of a clear alternative speedometer when driving on the Continent or when crossing the border between the United States and Canada is obvious. This secondary information is selected when the metric/imperial switch is used on the trip computer. This converts the displayed trip information to the appropriate local units at the same time.

The use of a vacuum fluorescent odometer display was made possible when legislation covering the use of non-volatile memories was agreed. Again removing the traditional barrel odometer from the main speedometer dial has helped to maintain the uncluttered presentation while giving an improved total mileage display to the driver.

The integration of modern displays for indicating battery state, oil pressure, coolant temperature and fuel level has presented the opportunity for giving the driver additional information associated with these functions. Firstly, any warning related to the state of the functions monitored by the gauges is displayed on the gauges themselves, thus limiting the amount of eye movement required by the driver to ascertain problems. Secondly, unlike conventional instruments, no red appears on the gauges until a warning state occurs. At that time red chaplets indicating the degree of the problem appear together with a red warning frame around the gauge identification symbol. The ability to flash the warning frame gives an additional level of hazard awareness if a function deteriorates further, for example the fuel gauge turns to red lower chaplets when the tank capacity drops to about 4.5 gallons; these red chaplets are accompanied by a static warning frame. When the fuel level drops further, to about 1.5 gallons, the red frame begins to pulse, emphasizing to the driver the immediate need to refuel.

3 THE DESIGN AND EVALUATION OF THE VEHICLE CONDITION MONITOR (VCM) DISPLAY

In the search to answer the problems of increasing numbers of warning lamps, coupled with the need for a flexible system, the design team developed what is probably the most innovative area on the driver display, *viz.* the VCM. The Styling Studio gradually refined its proposals until the final choice was made of a 32 × 32 dot matrix with its associated red and yellow/amber warning frame, backed up with a 14 segment 2 × 10 character message centre (Fig. 3). The choice of display provided a grid of sufficient resolution to adequately portray the ISO symbols and others designed by the company, and one which is compatible with the display and processor circuit technology being used. The func-

Fig. 3 The vehicle condition monitor assembly

tions monitored included brake malfunctions, fluid levels, lamp failures and seat belt use.

3.1 The aim

The aim of the evaluation and development work with the Institute for Consumer Ergonomics was to develop the best system available at that time and to assess potential problems of symbol recognition when using the dot matrix symbols compared with conventional ISO-based designs. It was also envisaged that the research programme would equip the company with experimental data to reinforce any requests for legislative change that may be necessary when considering the use of new technology.

As well as the ability to recognize the warning symbols and messages, it is important for the attention of the driver to be adequately attracted by the display while he or she is concentrating on the driving.

3.2 The experiments

The preliminary experiment to assess whether dot matrix symbols were as recognizable as conventional printed line symbols was conducted with 250 drivers, including 50 in pilot trials used to check experimental procedure. Subjects were selected from the general driving population and a range of ages and both sexes were represented. The range of eyesight was that expected in the general driving population and was tested in advance of the experiment.

Groups of five drivers were seated in front of a screen and symbols were presented to them as photographic representations in the form of coloured slides. Some of the potential symbols were available in ISO 2575 or as draft BSI standards. These, together with newly designed symbols to represent functions not covered by legislation, made up the 14 symbols which were evaluated in the initial test. The viewing distance from the screen and symbol height ensured that the angle subtended at the eye was the same as in normal driving. Hence the symbols were seen as the same size as if they had been presented in a car. The symbols were presented in dot matrix and conventional format using a pro-

jection tachistoscope and timer, to expose each slide for a specified time.

3.2.1 Learning phase

The subjects were shown each symbol with the appropriate legend in both formats. The symbol exposure time was 10 seconds. As each symbol and legend was shown the subjects ticked the corresponding legend on the response sheet. Each symbol and legend was shown twice during the learning phase.

3.2.2 Test phase

The subjects were shown each symbol in both formats but without the legends. The subjects had to tick the corresponding legend on the response sheet. The symbol exposure time was 300 ms; the response time 8 s. The exposure and response times had been established in pilot studies. The symbols were presented in random order. The first two complete sets of symbols were regarded as practice and the results were not scored. In the scored section each symbol was presented in random order five times, in both formats—a total of ten presentations.

Four versions of the response sheet were used in the experiment. The legends were presented in a different order in the four versions. This ensured that no one symbol would be more frequently recognized due to the position of the legend on the response sheet.

3.2.3 Comments phase

At the end of the test phase the symbols and legends in both formats were shown to the drivers and their comments noted.

The main experiments to evaluate the attention-getting qualities of the VCM display were conducted in a car rig in which the information displayed was simulated using a microcomputer. This part of the experiment was also utilized to test people's ability to use the trip computer successfully and over 100 drivers tested either the computer or the computer and VCM together.

Drivers sat in the car rig which simulated an XJ40 driving position and steered along a video road picture. At intervals they were required to use the trip computer and periodically a dot matrix warning symbol and message flashed up on the information display. Driver response to noticing the display was timed by using a foot switch which the subject had to press on seeing a warning. This warning then had to be identified verbally. A driver had to see, recognize and interpret warning displays quickly, without distracting his or her attention from the road.

It was not practical to measure eye movements in response to the presentation of a symbol as this required sophisticated and bulky equipment which would interfere with other functions in the driving task. However, the experimenters observed the drivers' response to the presentation of the symbols and it was noted that drivers correctly responded to the VCM symbols using very rapid eye movements to glance at the VCM display and back to the road.

3.3 The results

How well did the dot matrix format symbols compare with the conventional symbols?

An analysis of the number of errors was carried out for each symbol in both formats. The related samples 't' test was used to compare error rates. The results are shown graphically in Fig. 4.

In performance terms there was no significant difference between the two forms of presentation of the symbols. Drivers could recognize and match symbols with the appropriate legends equally well (or badly) whether the symbols were presented in dot matrix format or in conventional format. In subjective terms many drivers reported that the dot matrix format of symbols was more difficult to see clearly under the very fast viewing conditions imposed in this experiment.

There were few individual symbols which performed better or worse in dot matrix format compared with the conventional format. However, some drivers mentioned that the symbols with curves, particularly the BRAKE-related symbols, were less clear in dot matrix format. Some drivers considered that the OUTSIDE TEMP LOW symbol was more effective in dot matrix format.

About one-quarter of the drivers did not notice during the experiment that some symbols were dot matrix format and some were not. Some drivers noticed that certain symbols were less clear (that is the dot matrix ones) than others but did not realize the cause until the end of the test when the slides were re-presented. A more detailed paper dealing with this part of the test was delivered to the American Society of Automotive Engineers during February 1986 (3).

A very positive general response was shown by the great majority of drivers to the VCM. They considered the VCM to be a good idea in principle and well executed, and they used it accurately and quickly. The symbols were considered to be in a good position and were clear to read in the dot matrix format, of a satisfactory size and in many cases their meaning was obvious to the drivers.

It was considered desirable to display both symbols and messages. The messages were clear and easy to read and helped the drivers to differentiate between symbols. The symbols acted to attract the drivers' attention to the VCM.

Some drivers thought that too much information was provided and that some functions were not necessary (4).

4 THE DESIGN AND EVALUATION OF THE TRIP COMPUTER

After the decision to fit a trip computer had been made and the functions decided upon, new approaches were made to reduce the number of buttons and to present a keyboard with easily located buttons and logical sub-groups of functions which could be used with minimum interference when driving the vehicle. The principal components were three numerical input buttons and a range of nine functions which could be called up by pressing one of three dedicated buttons. The keyboard also contained the message CLEAR function, the unit selector, the memory clear (MC) function and the VCM showroom facility.

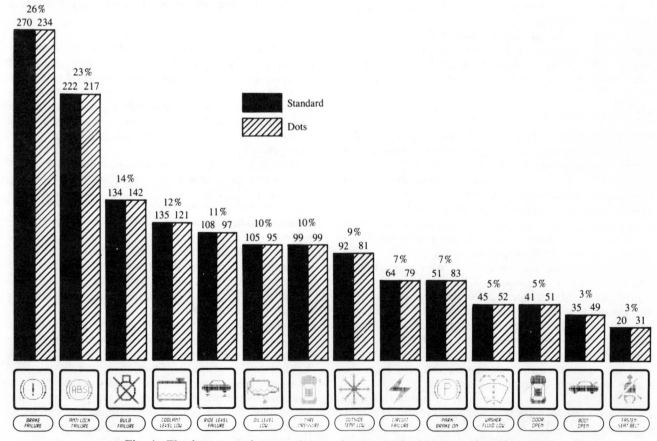

Fig. 4 The frequency of errors: dot matrix compared with conventional format

The decisions made in the choice of keyboard layout were later corroborated by the Institute in their testing and by research carried out by other people.

There are three main components in the use of a trip computer: data input, call-up of functions, and reading and understanding the displayed information.

The only data input required for this trip computer is the trip distance, entered at the beginning of a journey. Other information is collected automatically. Experiments by Heintz et al. (5) showed that for data input to a trip computer, a sequence keyboard such as that used in the trip computer took twice as long as a telephone keyboard to operate.

However, in 60 per cent of cases the drivers used the sequence keyboard without looking at the key locations, whereas this was only done in 15 per cent of cases using the telephone keyboard. Therefore, the sequence keyboard is less distracting than a keyboard with dedicated number keys. In the present tests no drivers reported any difficulty using the three-digit sequence keyboard to input trip distance.

Similarly, the advantages of using a sequence keyboard to call up trip information were reported by Heintz et al. (5). Although it took longer to press the keys using a sequence keyboard compared with a telephone keyboard the distraction effects appeared to be much less. It was clear from the results obtained in the three tests carried out by the Institute for Consumer Ergonomics (6) that the logic sequence plays a major role in the successful use of the trip computer.

4.1 The aims of the experiment

The ergonomic evaluation of the trip computer addressed three main areas:

(a) the keyboard layout,
(b) the messages displayed,
(c) the logic sequence linking the keyboard and the messages.

4.2 The experiment

One hundred drivers were used to test the trip computer by sitting them in the car rig and getting them to 'drive' along a video road picture.

At intervals they answered questions about the journey by using the trip computer, for example 'how far have we gone?' The number and location of key presses on the trip computer were recorded using the microcomputer and in addition experimenters observed the keyboard use and strategies adopted, such as hand/finger location. Each subject was also questioned about the use and acceptability of the information displayed.

During the experiment the results being obtained caused the design team to modify the logic sequences being used, and Table 1 illustrates how different displayed words and the position of functions in each sequence were progressed to reduce the number of errors made by drivers.

4.3 The results

4.3.1 Accuracy of use of the trip computer

Button press errors were generally low, approximately 10 per cent under stress conditions, but certain functions were highlighted as causing difficulty. For example, the multi-concept functions 'Distance on remaining fuel' and 'Average speed' producing higher errors, which were reduced in later tests, when the different logic patterns were introduced.

The general principles underlying the assessment and relocation of the functions of the trip computer were:

(a) the meaningfulness of the messages,
(b) the maintenance of a logic pattern in the sequences appearing on the three main functions: TIME, DISTANCE and FUEL,
(c) location of the most difficult functions first, in order to enhance learning and simplify location.

4.3.2 Strategies adopted when using the trip computer

The keyboard layout was very favourably received by the drivers. It was considered easy to use, the keys were easy to locate and discriminate and the keyboard was well positioned on the instrument panel. The angle and layout of the keyboard enhanced the positioning of the hand when using the keys.

Drivers either pressed the keys without supporting their hand (see Fig. 5a) or they rested their second and third fingers on the flat panel (see Fig. 5b) or they rested their fingers on the lower edge (see Fig. 5c).

The majority of drivers tried to identify patterns in the number of key presses.

Two main strategies for calling up a function were:

(a) to go immediately to the correct key and number of presses and then look at the message to check and read,
(b) to press the key once and look at the message and then repeat until the correct function was located.

Many drivers started with strategy (b) and moved to strategy (a) with practice.

Table 1 Trip computer logic sequences

Button	No. of presses	Message Test 1	Test 2	Test 3
DIST	1	DIST TRAV	DIST EMPTY	DIST EMPTY
DIST	2	FUEL FOR	DIST TRAV	DIST TRAV
DIST	3	DIST TO GO	DIST TO GO	DIST TO GO
FUEL	1	INST FUEL	FUEL USED	AV FUEL
FUEL	2	AV FUEL	INST FUEL	FUEL USED
FUEL	3	FUEL USED	AV FUEL	INST FUEL
TIME	1	TIME TAKEN	TIME TAKEN	AV SPEED
TIME	2	ARRIVAL	ARRIVAL	TIME TAKEN
TIME	3	AV SPEED	AV SPEED	TIME TO GO

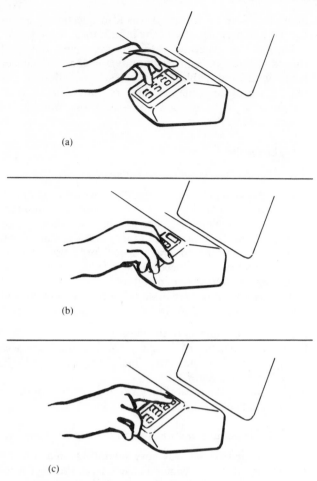

Fig. 5 Keyboard operating strategies

4.3.3 Trip computer functions

Drivers rated the usefulness on a five-point scale of the nine functions available on the trip counter. The logic sequence recommended after the tests (6) was closely aligned to this subjective assessment. A paper by Lopez (7) based on the opinions of experienced users of trip computers also corroborated the recommendations.

5 THE DESIGN AND EVALUATION OF THE ENVIRONMENTAL CONTROLS

The initial design proposals for the control panel were affected by two main inputs:

(a) the stereotype already used in existing company products,
(b) the additional functions and refinements needing to be controlled on the new unit.

In the latter consideration Jaguar now had a facility for humidity control, an important factor in overall driver comfort, particularly applicable on long journeys where dry, air conditioned atmospheres can affect fatigue and contribute to eye problems.

5.1 The aims

The ergonomic contribution to the controls took two forms. These were the development and testing of a symbol for humidity controls, and an assessment and refinement of the complete control panel (1, 2).

5.2 The experiment

5.2.1 The symbol

The first step was to identify a symbol to represent the concept of humidity.

Creativity groups composed of people who had all recently experienced a humid climate identified several humidity concepts. These humidity concepts were translated into symbol form and assessed by further similarly composed groups. The most satisfactory humidity symbol to emerge from the creativity groups was produced in four versions for test. The versions took account of outline and solid form, single and multiple form.

The four humidity symbols (see Fig. 6), together with eight other 'noise' symbols selected from Dreyfus' Symbol Source Book (1972), (8), formed the test material. These eight 'noise' symbols were chosen for similarity of concept or for similarity of form. Two hundred drivers tested these eight noise symbols and one of each of the four humidity symbols. The nine symbols and their labels were presented using a tachistoscope for an exposure time of 400 m/s. The order of presentation of the symbols was arranged such that each symbol had an equal chance of being first, second, third and so on.

After 45 minutes, during which time the subjects completed secondary tasks unrelated to symbols, they were required to match the nine symbols and labels. The results were analysed in terms of the number of people who accurately matched the symbols and labels and also the nature of any confusion errors.

5.2.2 The controls

The laboratory experiments on these items fell into three areas:

(a) an overall assessment of the basic design and the refining of the ideas to produce models for testing,

Fig. 6 Humidity symbols

(b) the need to identify the direction stereotype for increasing/decreasing humidity and include these results on the models,

(c) testing of the whole panel to assess the total design.

Phase (a) was completed through discussion between the company and the Institute and various recommendations were included in the models. These included modifying the layout to take advantage of direction stereotypes, for example heat should be increased by a clockwise rotation or left to right slider motion.

Phase (b) involved 120 drivers comprising equal numbers of men and women of a variety of ages. Two forms of humidity controls were involved in the experiment—a row of three push buttons and a three-position slider control. The controls were not labelled. The concept of making the air more or less humid was explained to the subjects. They were then told to imagine it was a VERY MUGGY DAY or a VERY DRY DAY. On a signal they were then required to MOVE THE SLIDER or PUSH THE BUTTON as quickly as possible using either their LEFT or their RIGHT hand in order to MAKE THE AIR DRIER or to ADD MORE MOISTURE TO THE AIR. The slider knob was always placed in the central position. The push buttons were momentary contact; therefore they gave no indication of position. The response schedule was arranged so that equal numbers of people

(a) used the push button or the slider control,
(b) started from moist or dry conditions,
(c) moved to drier or more moist conditions,
(d) used their right or left hand.

The experimenter noted the direction of operation of the slider control or the position of the button pressed.

This form of experimental design was used to overcome any bias in the responses. The data was analysed by computer using the OMNIBUS analysis of variance program and the Kruskal–Wallis test was employed.

Phase (c) again involved the use of two different models of the environmental control panel which were fitted in turn into a vehicle simulator. Forty-two drivers assessed the ease of operation of all the controls and the comprehensibility of the control labels. Each driver was asked to adjust the controls according to a particular scenario. Their actions and comments were noted on a recording schedule.

5.3 The results

5.3.1 Symbols

1. If only one symbol was to be used the most satisfactory was:

2. If a scale of symbols was to be used, the outline symbols were the most satisfactory;

3. Any of the forms of humidity symbol did as well or better than most of the comparator symbols; therefore, either form—solid or outline—would suffice when taking other considerations into account.

The size of the display area available plus the manufacturing methods to be employed caused us to use the solid form of water drop symbol (Fig. 6c).

5.3.2 Direction stereotype for humidity

The results of this part of the experiment were less conclusive in that the drivers appeared to react to the use of the controls by always moving the slider to the right or pressing any button irrespective of the scenario described to the participant. The main difficulty appears to be in the lack of understanding of the humidity concept by those taking part in the tests. Although slider controls appeared to give significantly better results in operation ($p < 0.05$) many of those tested stated their preference for the more high technology image presented by the push-button controls. Because of the use of a slider already on the panel, that is the face-level air distribution control, it was decided to use push buttons for the humidity functions. To emphasize the other advantages of completely switching off the unit, that is when full ambient humidity enters the car, the word ECON is used on the final button.

5.3.3 The whole panel test

As a result of the consumer tests refinements were made to the graphics, the shape of the large rotary controls, the position of some of the functions on those controls and the positioning of the manual/auto control in relation to the humidity buttons.

When introducing new features to the consumer, it is important to test their ability to use these functions successfully and the tests on the environment controls have given the company a firm basis for confidence of their layout in the vehicle.

6 AUTOSHIFT CONTROL

When discussing the displays and controls of the XJ40 mention must be made of the unique J-gate automatic gear shift and the design philosophy behind it.

The choice of high overdrive ratios provides a driving style that, while giving good fuel consumption figures, is not necessarily very sporting. Since it was wished to exploit the performance potential of the car the ability to operate the car in a pseudo-manual mode would be an advantage, and the engineers therefore sought to create a gear control that would achieve this and at the same time would be as free from the potential for mis-use as possible. Many systems that encourage the easy use of the lower gear retention facilities suffer from the possibility of inadvertent engagement of the reverse, park or neutral positions when changing back up to the normal D mode.

The provision of a reasonable separation between functions helps to overcome this problem but unfortunately leads to a very long shift action. The simple expediency of bending the gate into the J-shape has enabled the solution of both the problem of a lengthy action and the danger of inadvertent override when using the gears in a semi-manual mode. To help ensure that drivers do not leave the vehicle in any other mode than 'park' an audible warning has been added which is activated if the ignition keys are withdrawn when the gear selector is in any of the other positions.

A considerable amount of in-house evaluation has developed the J-gate to the fine levels of operation now available in the XJ40, and external evaluation has been carried out with the autoshift, as with all the features outlined in this paper, through the additional media of consumer clinics held in our major markets during the development programme of the vehicle. These clinics involved the subjective responses of a further 1412 prospective owners.

7 CONCLUSIONS

The ergonomic evaluation work that Jaguar has undertaken in conjunction with the Institute for Consumer Ergonomics Automotive Ergonomics Unit has progressed the instrumentation and controls of the XJ40 into the next evolution of the company's design philosophy for highly specified, driver-usable interiors.

The refinement of the systems has taken many man-hours of research, has involved over 600 drivers in the test programmes, and has produced results which have given us confidence in the acceptability and usability of the design. The long programme of research has moved from initial concept sketches, through mock-up interiors, user trials in the simulator and now has finally been evaluated on the road in the vehicle itself.

Testing novel vehicle instrumentation in a driving simulator rather than in road trials has the advantage that test subjects, experimenters and equipment are not put at risk. However, there are disadvantages, particularly if the novel instrumentation is not precisely that which would be found in real life, and if the effects of distracting the driver's attention are to be assessed. In the early tests it was not advisable to carry out road trials for two main reasons: the equipment for test was not readily available, and the amount of distraction arising from the novel instrumentation could not be predicted in advance, hence it could be hazardous.

In order to assess driver response to the information display, drivers were required to respond to a large number of events occurring quite frequently during the test period. In order to identify rapidly potential problems subjects were given only a brief familiarization with the equipment. They were also required to respond

at a pace set by the experimenter rather than at his or her own pace. Under these stressful conditions the number of errors associated with the use of the novel equipment were high. In normal driving the pattern of errors would probably be similar but the number of errors would be lower because the driver can set his own pace and think about the use of the equipment in advance. The most problematic call-up routines will still distract the driver's attention or his or her eyes from the road. The aim has been to minimize this distraction by satisfactory design. Consideration of these factors has also been made by Mackie (9), Greene and Sendelbach (10) and Cilibraise (11) reporting on current states-of-the-art.

It is most important that novel facilities such as trip computers, driver information systems, and the operating controls of other new features should be easy to interpret and use. Drivers should not be distracted from their main task of driving the vehicle safely and any information given them must be useful and accessible. The tests have given the company a high degree of confidence in having achieved this objective.

In addition data have been collected which have been useful in the preparation of the instruction manuals and the tapes for driving information, and other results from the tests have provided the company with valuable insights into future design possibilities for inclusion on the next generation of interiors.

REFERENCES

1 **Galer, M. D.** and **Spicer, J.** An ergonomics assessment of Jaguar instrumentation. Institute for Consumer Ergonomics, confidential report to Jaguar Cars Limited, 1981.

2 **Galer, M. D., Spicer, J.** and **Geyer, T. A. W.** An ergonomics assessment of Jaguar instrumentation. Final report, Institute for Consumer Ergonomics, Confidential report to Jaguar Cars Limited, 1983.

3 **Galer, M. D., Holtum, C.** and **Spicer, J.** The recognition and readability of dot matrix warning symbols in cars. SAE International Congress and Exposition, 1986, SAE paper 860180.

4 **Galer, M. D., Geyer, T. A. W., Spicer, J.** and **Holtum, C.** The design and evaluation of a trip computer and vehicle condition monitor display. Fourth International Conference on *Automotive electronics*, 1983, paper C229/83 (Institution of Electrical Engineers, London).

5 **Heintz, F., Haller, R.** and **Bouis, D.** Safer trip computers by human factors design. SAE International Congress and Exposition, 1982, SAE paper 820105.

6 **Geyer, T. A. W., Spicer, J.** and **Galer, M. D.** Experiments on a proposed design of in-vehicle trip computer. Institute for Consumer Ergonomics, confidential report to Jaguar Cars Limited, 1982.

7 **Lopez, L. A.** Growth and development of electronic display information systems. Third International Conference on *Automotive electronics*, 1981, paper C201/81 (Mechanical Engineering Publications, London).

8 **Dreyfus, H.** *Symbol source book*, 1972 (McGraw-Hill, New York).

9 **Mackie, C.** Vehicle condition monitoring and electronic instrument displays. Third International Conference on *Automotive electronics*, 1981, paper C175/81 (Mechanical Engineering Publications, London).

10 **Greene, E. S.** and **Sendelbach, D. R.** Definition of driver information instrumentation features. SAE International Congress and Exposition, 1980, SAE paper 800353.

11 **Cilibraise, G.** The second generation family of Ford trip computers—the Tripminder. SAE International Congress and Exposition, 1982, SAE paper 820107.

The design and development of the XJ40 seating system

M J Arrowsmith, CEng, MIMechE, MIProdE
Jaguar Cars Limited, Coventry

This paper describes the research, design and development processes involved in the creation of the Jaguar XJ40 seating system.

1 INTRODUCTION

The objective in designing and developing a completely new seating system for the XJ40 was to further improve upon the current products' standards of comfort, durability and appearance to maintain a lead over competition for the life of the model.

2 RESEARCH

Before embarking upon the design of a completely new seat, it was considered prudent to assess the current Series III saloon seat for comfort levels, to consider its design features in the light of published ergonomic information and above all to discover the customer's opinion of the seat. This exercise was carried out on behalf of Jaguar by the Vehicle Ergonomics Group at Loughborough University.

The exercise included a literature survey and a postal questionnaire from which drivers' comments on seat features and levels of perceived comfort were collated. The questionnaire was also completed by the company's test drivers.

Since comparison of comfort levels is notoriously difficult owing to the subjectivity of assessment and the wide range of stature and posture encountered, a reliable method of measurement was required. A technique was devised whereby a group of subjects representing both sexes, a variety of social and economic groups and the 5th–95th percentile stature range was used to assess the various seating positions in a Series III saloon. At various intervals the subjects were asked to rate comfort using the scale shown for the body areas indicated on Fig. 1. Subjects were first questioned after 15 minutes sitting in the car in order to assess the showroom condition, then again after 30 minutes driving to represent a short test drive, followed by half-hour intervals during an extended test drive of one and a half hours.

The correlation between the experimental results obtained and the opinion surveys was good; this technique was therefore used for all subsequent measurement work. Although the results were favourable overall, several areas of potential improvement were highlighted, and these were incorporated into the Series III design.

The changes made were only minor yet they had a significant effect on passenger comfort. For instance the piping across the front edge of the cushion was lowered to reduce contact with the underside of the thigh; this feature was carried over on to the XJ40. Secondly, the rear of the cushion was stiffened by reducing the size of the cavities in the foam. This part of the cushion supports the bulk weight of the torso (see Fig. 2) through the ischial tuberosities which are the bony protruberances at the base of the buttocks. The cushion generally has the thinnest section here due to the rake of the top surface; as a result, on the XJ40 no cavities are incorporated in this area.

The effectiveness of these changes was demonstrated by the results of a further assessment exercise. This illustrated the value of the changes and provided valuable data for the XJ40 seat profile.

Both the surveys and the experimental work also confirmed that seat height adjustment as well as fore and aft and squab recline, in conjunction with steering wheel fore and aft adjustment, is essential to provide a comfortable posture for the full range of stature.

In order to develop guidelines for the suspension of the XJ40 seats, an investigation into the dynamic behaviour of the Series III seats was undertaken on behalf of the company by the Advanced Vehicle Technology Group of BL Technology.

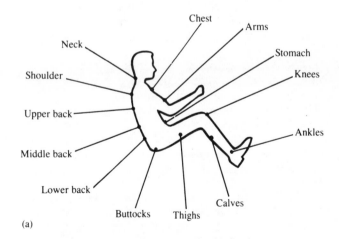

(a)

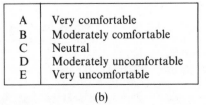

A	Very comfortable
B	Moderately comfortable
C	Neutral
D	Moderately uncomfortable
E	Very uncomfortable

(b)

Fig. 1 Body and seat comfort questionnaire (a) body areas rated (b) comfort ratings

0265-1904/86 $2.00 + .05

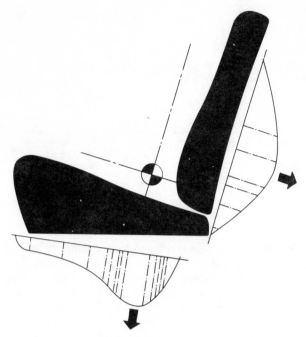

Fig. 2   Typical load distribution

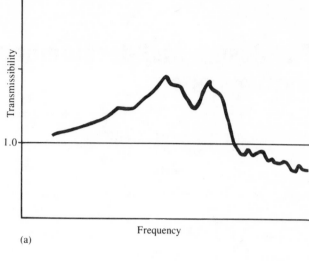

(a)

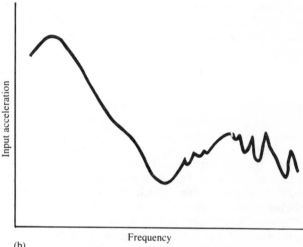

(b)

Fig. 3   Graphs of frequency versus (a) transmissibility and (b) acceleration

Test work was carried out over a variety of known road surfaces representing motorway, A roads, B roads and unclassified roads to represent the full range of normal driving conditions. Vibration was measured using accelerometers, recording only vertical accelerations which were positioned in the front and rear footwell and at the occupant–seat interfaces. The signals were recorded on magnetic tape and then calibrated and stored on a computer disc for subsequent plotting. The magnetic tape was used to drive an electro-hydraulic rig to enable laboratory simulation of tests for development purposes. The vehicle was run either two up or weighted to the gross vehicle weight condition. The two occupants were chosen to illustrate the different response obtained between heavy and light passengers.

From the data graphical plots of the vehicle response and transmissibility were obtained (Fig. 3), where transmissibility is the ratio of vehicle input to occupant.

The results for the front seats showed that for most of the test conditions the troughs on the transmissibility curve were coincident with peaks on the input curve, which is ideal. It was interesting to note, however, that the transmissibility with the lighter occupants was significantly higher.

The results for the rear seat showed higher vehicle inputs and also higher transmissibility ratios (an increase of between 13.6 and 32.9 per cent). Additionally troughs of transmissibility did not match peaks of input. Overall this represents a significantly poorer rear seat ride than front. It should be borne in mind of course that the Series III ride is widely regarded by other manufacturers as the target to strive for.

The significant difference in performance between front and rear can be attributed to the different seat suspension systems. The front seat consists of a foam pad supported by a rubber diaphragm (Fig. 4), both of which materials have inherent damping properties. The

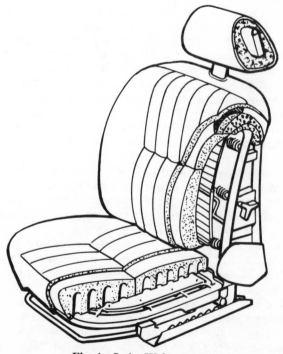

Fig. 4   Series III front seat

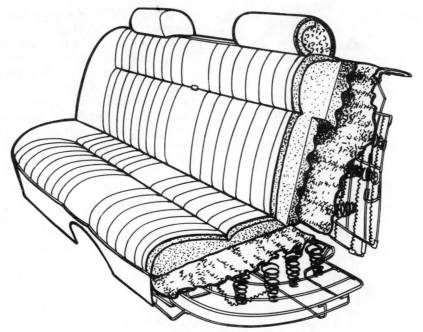

Fig. 5   Series III rear seat

rear seat, however, is of steel sprung construction (Fig. 5), with virtually no damping.

3 DESIGN

The foregoing research work gave clear direction for the design of the XJ40 seating system, leading to the decision to use a full depth foam for the rear seat using the body seat pan as a base (Fig. 6).

For the front seats, where seat adjustment mechanisms had to be packaged under the cushion, a rubber diaphragm was chosen to support the foam (Fig. 7).

Cushion and squab profiles were based on the modified version of the Series III.

'Cold cure' polyurethane foam was chosen rather than rubberized hair or latex foam since it is light, has good repeatability of form and its hardness and density can readily be adjusted to tune for seat comfort.

Tubular, pressed steel or plastics construction was possible for the frame of the seat. However, the shorter lead time, lower tool costs and known safety characteristics led to the choice of a tubular frame as in the Series III. This had the further advantages of ease of incorporation of variants or possible modifications during the development process.

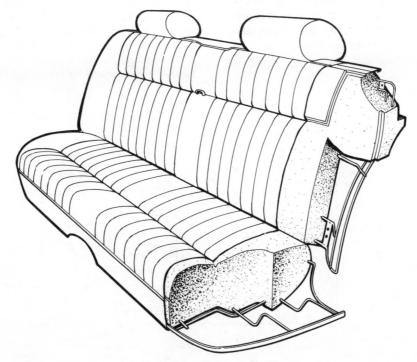

Fig. 6   XJ40 rear seat

Fig. 7   XJ40 front seat

High-strength steel was used for early prototypes but the weight-saving advantage was minimal compared to the difficulty experienced by the manufacturers in maintaining tolerances. The decision was therefore taken to revert to mild steel. (Maintaining close tolerances is important since the alignment of recline mechanisms and seat slides is controlled by their mounting on the frame.)

Naturally, electric seat adjustment on certain variants was necessary for a car of this class. Fore and aft motion and rise and fall of front and rear of the seat was achieved by packaging motors and mechanisms beneath the cushion. Electric recline was provided by a mechanism and motor situated in the squab.

A critical datum point known as the H point depends upon the seat design (Fig. 8). It is intended to represent the position of the hip joint of a theoretical passenger and from this point critical items, such as screen wiped area, rear view mirror visibility, head room and pedal positions, are dimensioned.

Its position is measured by placing a standard weighted mannikin (Fig. 9) on the seat and measuring the coordinates of the hip joint centre. As it depends to a large extent on the deflection of the seat suspension it has to be determined experimentally to validate the design. Subsequent tuning of the seat suspension during the development process has to be carefully controlled to avoid losing this datum position.

The design decisions were based on sound practical research work and it is interesting to note that the outcome was a logical evolution of the Series III seat.

4 DEVELOPMENT

On completion of design prototype tooling was laid down and seats built to equip the extensive test fleet. From vehicles on test in Arizona, Canada, Australia and the United Kingdom, coupled with numerous management appraisals, the company was soon able to draw on a wide range of driver reports.

These initial results were not as promising as expected. In particular there was fairly frequent criticism of inadequate lateral support and excessive lumbar pressure in the front seats. Additionally 'submarining' was evident in the rear, that is the tendency for the passengers to slide down the squab or vertical portion of the seat and forward along the cushion. A comfort evaluation exercise was carried out by the Vehicle Ergonomics Group which substantiated these reports.

During this period of development 'clinics' were being held both in the United Kingdom and the United States. In this process selected individuals appraised the vehicle in controlled conditions to assess customer reaction to the vehicle concept and styling. From these 'clinics' it became apparent that the styling theme of the seats in particular was not as traditional as generally desired.

As a direct result of the clinic reports a restyling exercise was carried out to revert to a more traditional seat trim style. This was mainly achieved by changing from the original XJ40 lateral flutes (Fig. 10) to vertical flutes similar to the Series III (Fig. 11).

Advantage of the change was taken to undertake further development of seat comfort (Fig. 12). The verti-

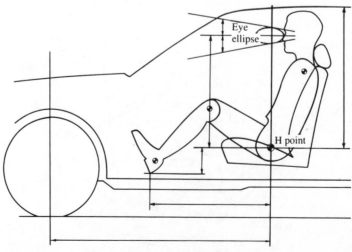

Fig. 8   H point related dimensions

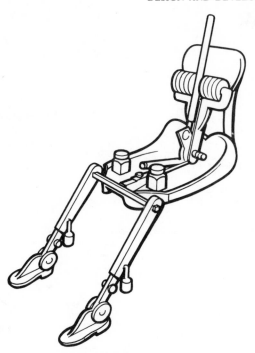

Fig. 9 H point mannikin

Fig. 11 Final XJ40 style

cal fluting allowed a more concave squab section in both front and rear seats which improved lateral support, which was originally limited by the tendency of the lateral flutes to wrinkle. At the same time the hardness of the squab foams was reduced. This again improved lateral support due to additional deflection and it also corrected lumbar pressure.

Further improvement to lumbar support was made by using a mechanical adjustment system in place of the screw-tensioned strap incorporated in the original design (Fig. 13). With the mechanical system the profile of the cross-bar accentuates pressure on the outer areas of the back, whereas the original system applied pressure to the centre of the lumbar area.

A small increase in foam hardness of the cushion marginally raised the sitting position. This had the effect of reducing the interference between the underneath of the front end of the thighs and the front of the cushion. It also positioned the torso more correctly to coincide with the lumbar feature of the squab.

To reduce the 'submarining' reported in the rear seat, it was only necessary to slightly increase cushion rake, which gave a further improvement in the torso–thigh angle (Fig. 14).

To establish the effect of these changes a further comfort evaluation was carried out by The Vehicle Ergonomics Group. In the exercise three competitors' vehicles were assessed for comparison.

The result of this comparison showed that not only had a very substantial gain in comfort been achieved

Fig. 10 Original XJ40 style

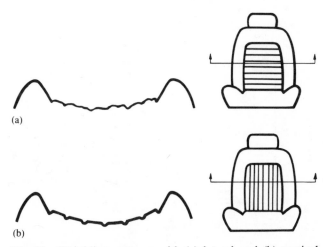

Fig. 12 Wrinkling patterns with (a) lateral and (b) vertical flutes

Fig. 13   Lumbar support mechanism

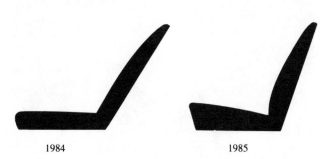

1984   1985

Fig. 14   Rear seat rakes

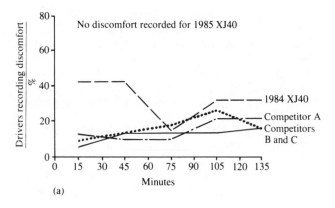

Fig. 15   Driver's seat comfort analysis (a) lower back and (b) right buttock

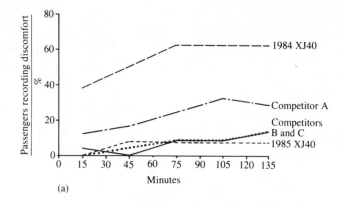

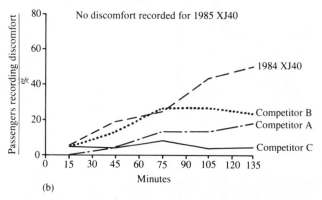

Fig. 16   Rear seat comfort analysis (a) lower back and (b) right buttock

relative to the original version of the seat but that in almost all aspects of seat comfort it was considered superior to its closest competitor (Figs 15 and 16).

Some teething problems with the seat adjustment mechanism were experienced during the early stages of development. In particular judder was experienced on rearward travel of the seat. This was resolved by a design change in which the long tightly radiused cable drives of the original mechanism were eliminated by repositioning the motors and driving lead nuts instead of lead screws. Some further problems existed with low-temperature operation ($-30°C$) but these were resolved by lead nut material changes and detail modification to thread dimensions.

Difficulties can occur on seat adjustment mechanisms due to the necessity for accurate alignment. This was the case particularly with the manual seat recline mechanisms. Misalignment initially created very high handwheel loads. The problem was resolved by attention to jigging of the seat frame and also a change from high-strength steel to mild steel to avoid spring back as previously mentioned in Section 3.

5 DURABILITY

The seats and their components were subjected to the company's standard range of material and rig endurance tests.

All variants of the seat were used in the $5\frac{1}{2}$ million miles of endurance vehicle running in the United Kingdom and at overseas test sites. They were found to be completely satisfactory even in the most arduous conditions for trim materials—the high temperatures and high ultraviolet radiation in Arizona and the −40°C temperatures of a Canadian arctic winter.

6 CONCLUSION

Sound guidelines were generated by the research work which allowed confident design decisions. Nevertheless a considerable amount of development work followed to ensure that comfort, durability and refinement objectives were met. This demonstrates that particularly where ergonomic considerations are important a certain amount of iterative work is unavoidable.

The achievement of these objectives was vividly demonstrated by the latest comfort assessment which showed that the product had improved on existing high standards.

ACKNOWLEDGEMENTS

The author wishes to acknowledge the valuable work on comfort assessment by Dr M. Porter and Mr M. Stearn of the Vehicle Ergonomics Group, Loughborough University of Technology, and also the assessments of seat dynamic behaviour by Mr P. Fleming of Gaydon Technology.

The utilization of fatigue life prediction techniques in support of a major vehicle project

C J Tivey, BA
Jaguar Cars Limited, Coventry

In this paper the techniques of fatigue life predictions are discussed along with decision paths that were necessary to enable design and development of the Jaguar XJ40 front suspension to take place.

1 INTRODUCTION

The dynamic behaviour of vehicles has become extremely important in recent years to meet the increased demands in structural performance, reliability, noise and safety requirements.

Engineers are faced with many decisions in the design and evaluation of a sophisticated motor car to ensure that it will resist fatigue failures.

This paper explains fatigue and gives examples of the logical decision path utilizing modern testing techniques which Jaguar used for developing the new product.

The motor vehicle is almost unique in the variety of duties expected of it from a totally uncontrolled population of users. This paper also outlines some of the requirements in defining the service history to ensure a durable and reliable product.

2 WHAT IS FATIGUE?

For some designers, the word fatigue is associated with a very complicated scientific approach using a highly theoretical approach and long mathematical equations. This is a misconception: the basic facts are very simple and knowledge of them can save time, material and money.

For other designers, fatigue does not exist, because their structures have been so overdesigned that nothing will break them. This may be satisfying, but is also expensive.

It is uncompetitive today to overdesign. There is enough information available to make a critical design possible and fatigue failure is likely only if the basic rules are disregarded.

Components may be stressed to just below their yield strength under a static load condition without a failure occurring. When the load fluctuates, the maximum permissible strength reduces.

Fatigue in materials, therefore, is the process by which repeated applications of a load less than the one needed to break a component by a single application eventually leads to the mechanical failure of that component.

In this section, a global view of the vehicle process is discussed and the engineering design/development process is investigated in more detail.

An effective development process is not possible without knowing what the vehicle will experience in its lifetime; this is discussed later.

Figure 1 depicts the product development cycle. This chart indicates how the process is really continuous in nature and the end of one design cycle is the beginning of the next. Generally, a new vehicle design is evolved from an existing one.

From the use of existing current models and market forecasts there arises an obvious need for change. The initial concept frequently begins with a definition of the customer needs recognized from existing products. This is progressed into the product plan for the vehicle. At this point it is important to have a good understanding of the vehicle's service history.

Service history is shown in the centre of the chart since it relates directly or indirectly to all phases of the product development cycle. The engineering design/development block in the diagram is the key element for relating service loads so that the process can proceed to

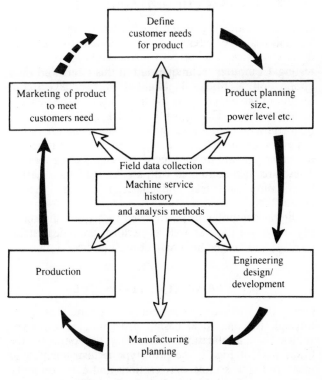

Fig. 1 Product development cycle

0265-1904/86 $2.00 + .05

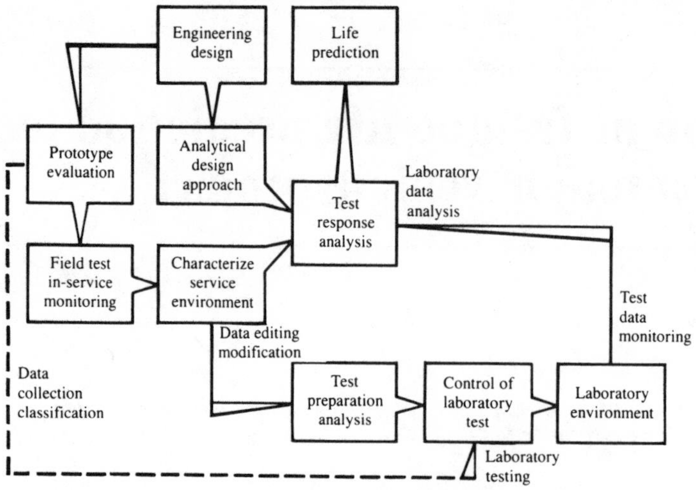

Fig. 2　Functional diagram design and analysis

the manufacturing, planning, production and sales of the product. This then has described the importance of service load data to each area in the implementation of a new vehicle.

A major goal in engineering design is to predict the service life of a component as early as possible. This is a major reason for the strong links between designer and development. The designer has both analytical and experimental tools available for assessing the fatigue durability of a component or part.

The diagram shown in Fig. 2 illustrates typical information processing tasks and paths for a fatigue evaluation. The task and flow of engineering data for analytical life prediction techniques encompass the upper portion of the figure. The lower part shows the major functions in the use of experimental techniques for service history simulation.

3　ANALYTICAL TECHNIQUES

Often in engineering design programmes, life prediction analysis can be integrated with design to optimize fatigue service life prior to undertaking durability testing. Computer techniques aid in this effort and their application is briefly highlighted in the next major section of the paper, using the front beam of the new car as an example. The upper loop of Fig. 2 denotes the major functions in assessing fatigue life using analytical design procedures. The drawings and model of a particular component are produced by engineering design. These are then combined with service load information from component test and material data to predict fatigue life.

Digital computer tasks are used to acquire and classify in-service data as well as perform analytical stress analysis and fatigue life prediction using these data.

4　EXPERIMENTAL TECHNIQUES

Once the vehicle component or system has gone through the analytical design procedure, a prototype vehicle is manufactured. Following the path in the lower part of Fig. 2, the prototype is instrumented to measure loads, strains, accelerations and displacements, and data are collected and stored onto magnetic tape

for a variety of proving ground and public road surfaces.

Computer techniques are then used to edit, display and analyse the data. The alternatives and details of applying these techniques in the overall process are discussed in the next section of the paper. During laboratory testing, the response of test specimens is also monitored and the data analysed in a similar manner.

4.1　Fatigue evaluation for typical vehicle components

As discussed previously, there are two complimentary approaches that can be applied to component fatigue assessment—those of life prediction analysis and service simulation testing (1).

This section uses a typical component to illustrate the alternatives. A front beam life prediction analysis is described as well as its associated durability programme.

4.2　Fatigue life prediction analysis

Current trends in the market place, together with government legislation, have created an urgent need to reduce both the cost and weight of automotive components.

In the development of previous front suspensions, the design has been based primarily on the basis of static considerations related to simple load cases and material properties such as ultimate tensile strength and proof stress.

In the automotive industry, design philosophies based on these concepts are generally unrealistic. The simple rules and design sheets derived, therefore, have very limited applicability in the variable-amplitude cyclic loading situation under which most components operate in service.

Cost effective designs require quantification of the performance of components and systems. The important parameters and factors which must be considered in the design process are stress and strain, deformation and deflection, and durability and performance, all of which must take into account costs and weight.

With reference to a new front suspension and the requirement for a new front beam, the following briefly outlines the design optimization that was carried out, and subsequently discusses the requirement for component testing.

A stress distribution that is balanced throughout the front beam is desirable. Stress concentrations such as those associated with discontinuities and sharp transitions must be avoided. The stiffness of the beam must be adequate to ensure that deflections under load will not adversely affect the operational behaviour of the vehicle (for example ride and handling characteristics). The design of the beam in terms of shape and material must ensure satisfactory durability.

The critical factors affecting performance can therefore be summarized as *load, shape* and *materials*.

Finally, all the aforementioned must be achieved at the right cost, weight and size.

4.2.1 Service loads

If we consider the loads and paths into the front beam, the following are of particular interest: force inputs from suspension arms, engine mounts, anti-roll bar, springs, dampers, the mounting on the body and the steering gear.

Service load measurement exercises were undertaken using specially built load cells to measure load in three directions at suspension location positions. These loads were used to develop load spectra for various vehicle weight conditions and to establish an understanding of the effect of the suspension on the strain distribution throughout the front beam.

4.2.2 Component shape

The strains and deformation in the front beam due to the loads are dictated by the component shape. To gain confidence in the ability of computer models to faithfully reflect front beam behaviour, parallel, theoretical and experimental exercises were carried out.

A finite element model using the linear elastic capability of NASTRAN was created using the load data previously recorded. The complete model is shown in Fig. 3a and b.

In parallel, a rig which could apply the loads statically to the beam was designed, manufactured and built. The rig simulated the vehicle installation and included all the hardware associated with the beam, that is suspension, steering linkages, stub axles etc. A brittle lacquer coating technique was used to highlight areas of highest strain. The beam was loaded and the lacquer cracked. From the crack patterns, strain gauges were placed in strategic positions and strain distributions and deflections measured.

The experimental results were compared with those of the finite element analysis, and the model tuned to give faithful reproduction.

4.2.3 Basic material data

The material used for the beam is a cold rolled general purpose steel. Monotonic properties for the steel and for most materials are usually easily obtainable. However, the cyclic properties are the only ones required for accurate fatigue life prediction work and this will be discussed in detail in the next section.

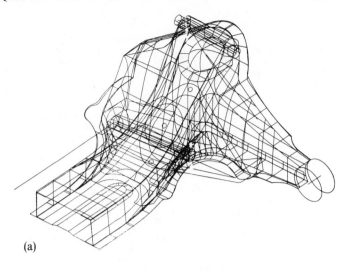

(a)

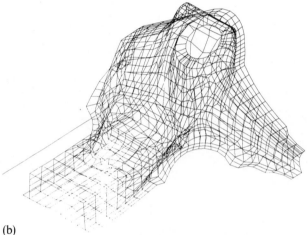

(b)

Fig. 3 Finite element model for the front beam

4.3 Durability assessment

The block diagram shown in Fig. 4 illustrates the basic elements of the fatigue life prediction process used. The fatigue analysis routine utilized the local stress–strain approach accepted by the experts as one of the most accurate techniques currently available (**2**).

The concepts of local stress–strain fatigue analysis have been developed over many years. Continuing research has provided confidence in the accuracy of the analysis techniques for a wide range of materials and components. The wider application of local stress–strain fatigue analysis has become possible because inexpensive but powerful computer systems and mass storage devices have become available.

Fatigue analysis of a component requires an accurate description of its service environment, accurate materials data and a fatigue analysis method of proven accuracy.

It is not the intention of this paper to go into great technical detail on the actual concepts of local stress–strain techniques but more to describe how the company has harnessed the technique to improve its vehicles.

Briefly, the analysis consists of cycle counting of data to extract closed fatigue cycles using a technique called 'rainflow', modelling the stress–strain response of the material, covering nominal strains to local strains, calculation of the fatigue damage on a cycle-by-cycle basis

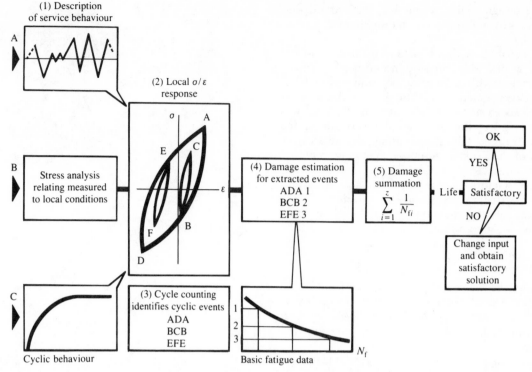

(1) Description of service behaviour

(2) Local σ/ε response

(4) Damage estimation for extracted events
ADA 1
BCB 2
EFE 3

(5) Damage summation $\sum_{i=1}^{z} \dfrac{1}{N_{fi}}$

OK

YES

Satisfactory

NO

Change input and obtain satisfactory solution

Stress analysis relating measured to local conditions

(3) Cycle counting identifies cyclic events
ADA
BCB
EFE

Cyclic behaviour

Basic fatigue data

Fig. 4 Schematic of fatigue life prediction process

using the Smith, Topper and Watson parameter (**3**) and finally summating the fatigue damage using Miner's rule (**4**).

5 INPUTS TO THE FATIGUE ANALYSIS

5.1 The description of the service environment

The fatigue analysis requires a time history of strain variations at the critical location in the component. This, in the case of the front beam, was obtained from strain gauges placed in critical locations highlighted by the brittle lacquer exercise. The time history was obtained by fitting the strain gauged component to a vehicle and collecting data from proving ground and public road services and recording the information on a magnetic tape for future 'off-line' analysis.

5.2 Stress analysis relating measured to local conditions

Fatigue cracks initiate in regions of local plasticity, usually at stress concentrations.

The stress–strain conditions at the stress–concentration are 'local' conditions and 'nominal' conditions apply away from the stress concentration. In most cases, the service environment strain is nominal hence a factor is required to relate nominal to local conditions. This factor, K_f, can be found from previous experimental data or from textbooks such as Peterson (**5**).

5.3 Materials data

The local strain approach requires seven parameters to describe cyclic material behaviour, four to establish a fatigue damage curve and three to define a cyclic stress–strain curve. For the purpose of fatigue life assessment, these data may be obtained in one of three ways:

1. *By direct measurement.* Methods for determining the required material properties are well documented and many laboratories now perform the necessary strain controlled fatigue tests.

Typical examples of a cyclic stress–strain curve and a strain–life curve are shown in Figs 5 and 6. Clearly, if maximum accuracy is required, then there is no substitute for obtaining these material parameters by direct measurement for the material of interest.

2. *From indirect measurement and calculation.* Approximation methods for the calculation of fatigue properties from more easily measurable parameters have been developed for situations where direct measurement is impractical. However, the results may not always be reliable, and these techniques should only be used for general assessments and comparisons, rather than for accurate fatigue life calculations.

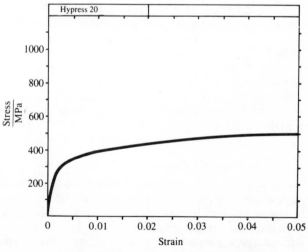

Fig. 5 Cyclic stress–strain curve

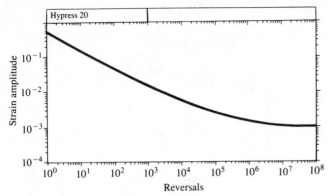

Fig. 6   Strain–life curve

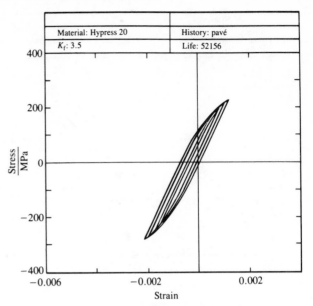

Fig. 7   Stress–strain hysteresis loops

3. *From existing databases.* As with service data, material data can be organized on a computer database form. Unlike service data, however, material information is common to many industries so that over the past fifteen to twenty years much information has been accumulated, covering, perhaps, 300–400 materials.

The materials data serves two functions. It provides an efficient means for storing and retrieving large quantities of data and it also makes the data for each material available to the fatigue analysis programmes. These two functions provide very powerful facilities for the efficient and rapid evaluation of alternative candidate materials and for investigating the sensitivity of the analysis to variations in material properties. The engineer is, therefore, provided with a realistic and logical material selection methodology.

6 OUTPUTS FROM THE FATIGUE ANALYSIS SYSTEM

The major objectives in the engineering application of local strain analysis are:

(a) to model the fatigue failure process for a given signal and material at the critical location within a component,
(b) to identify the fatigue damaging cycles in the strain time record,
(c) to evaluate the effects of design and material changes on fatigue life.

To meet these objectives, the company's analysis function provides adequate numerical and graphical outputs to enable the results to be interpreted correctly. Facilities for 'what if' evaluations are available and a number of design and material options can be assessed efficiently.

The following forms of output have been found valuable:

1. A graphical output of the most significant and damaging stress–strain hysteresis loops. These displays are particularly useful for comparing and understanding material effects (Fig. 7).
2. Displays of the distribution of fatigue cycles and damage against signal characteristics, such as range and mean. These displays may be used to identify the actual service events responsible for a particular fatigue process (Figs 8 and 9).
3. Output illustrating the effects of rescaling the input service history on fatigue life (Fig. 10).

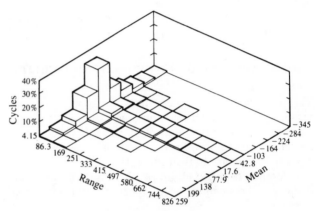

Fig. 8   Cycle plot

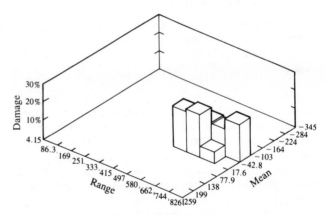

Fig. 9   Damage plot

These provide a useful quantitative guide to the degree of design alteration required to provide an adequate fatigue life.

Efficient and reliable computer-based fatigue life prediction methods now exist at Jaguar. Extensive software routines have been developed and implemented to exploit these techniques. This makes rapid assessment of design changes possible. By use of these techniques, the designer is able to select the optimum combination

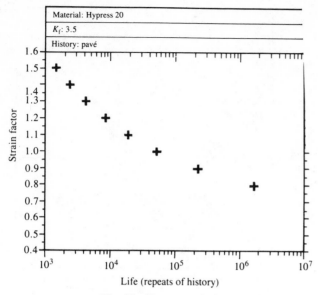

Fig. 10   Factor analysis

of material and shape to ensure satisfactory durability at the right cost, weight and size by evaluating a range of possibilities.

7 DEVELOPMENT OF COMPONENT DURABILITY TESTS

The approaches and alternatives in applying testing techniques for evaluating component durability can be assessed through utilization of a series of decision path guidelines, to establish the durability of redesigns and to develop confidence in their integrity.

Reference to Figs 11 to 14 illustrates the decisions made and being made to establish realistic test programmes.

7.1 Establish test objectives

The initial step in designing a test programme is clear communication of the test objectives between the designer and the test engineer. A decision path for aiding the process of communication is shown in Fig. 11.

In the case of the front beam an 'average' in-service environment was known for certain applications. Therefore, a field-related life estimate test was possible. However, the greatest unknown was still the total service environment; therefore, further data measurement using comparative tests on servo-hydraulic rigs were undertaken between existing and new components.

7.2 Establish test specimen

Generally, the smaller the specimen, the less expensive the test equipment for mechanical testing. It is important to note, however, that as the size of the specimen is reduced the finesse to conduct the test usually increases. Figure 12 illustrates a decision path to establish the test specimen.

In the case of the front beam, static tests identified that the beam cannot be simply isolated and the system, including suspension, had to be considered. In other words, a sub-structure was required.

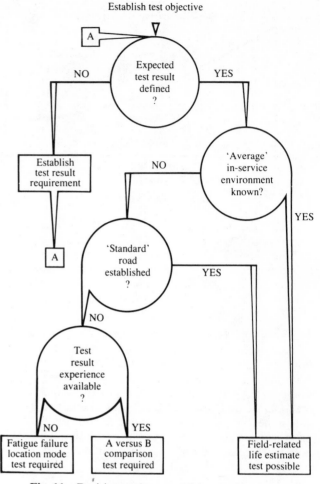

Fig. 11   Decision path to establish test objectives

7.3 Establish data collection locations

Once the test specimen is chosen, the data collection locations for simulated service histories can be determined. Digital computers are utilized to store service history data banks. Information is characterized accord-

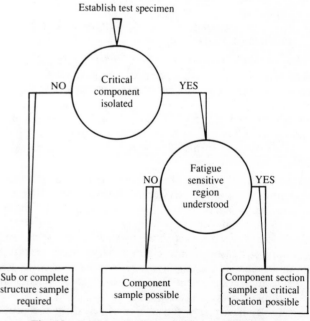

Fig. 12   Decision path to establish test specimen